Productivity and Innovation in SMEs

This book analyses the determining factors behind productivity and innovation amongst Small and Medium Enterprises (SMEs) in Singapore, and within the context of South East Asia, in order to offer recommendations for increasing productivity and aiding economic growth.

SME firms are an influential driver of economic growth in advanced world economies like the USA, Germany, Japan and South Korea. Throughout the 2000s, Singapore experienced a decline in economic growth which was linked to decreasing productivity in its SMEs. The decline triggered a transformational policy by a Government intent on forging a 'high skill–high productivity' future. Given substantial evidence that low productivity growth occurred in sectors where immigrants dominated the workforce, the seeds of recovery focused on improving productivity and innovation amongst SMEs in those sectors. Hence, this book investigates the factors determining productivity amongst SMEs across the manufacturing sector. It utilises personal interviews with global experts and CEOs, combined with primary data collected from a major international Delphi survey, and interviews with 215 SME owners and managers in Singapore. This data helps us to better understand how these productivity-enhancing factors can be used to increase performance amongst SMEs. By investigating the nature and process of total factor productivity in Singapore's SMEs, this book tells the policy story behind the revolution. To provide a comparative analysis, Singapore's story is placed within a South East Asian context. The unfolding narrative contains important lessons for policy makers and industry globally, as they assess the strategic choices available to them for improving productivity and innovation.

This book will be of great interest to students and scholars of innovation and productivity, as well as economic development officers, government policy advisors, SME business managers and sustainable businesses.

Azad Singh Bali is a Lecturer in Public Policy at the University of Melbourne.

Peter McKiernan is Professor of Management at the University of Strathclyde, Scotland.

Christopher Vas is Associate Professor at Murdoch University, Australia, and Deputy Dean and Director of the Singapore Centre for Research in Innovation, Productivity and Technology (SCRIPT).

Peter Waring is Associate Professor at Murdoch University, Australia, and Dean of the Singapore campus.

Routledge Focus on Environment and Sustainability

For more information about this series, please visit: www.routledge.com/
Routledge-Focus-on-Environment-and-Sustainability/book-series/RFES

Productivity and Innovation in SMEs

Creating Competitive Advantage in Singapore and South East Asia

Azad Bali, Peter McKiernan, Christopher Vas and Peter Waring

LONDON AND NEW YORK

First published 2019
by Routledge
2 Park Square, Milton Park, Abingdon, Oxon OX14 4RN

and by Routledge
52 Vanderbilt Avenue, New York, NY 10017

Routledge is an imprint of the Taylor & Francis Group, an informa business

© 2019 Azad Bali, Peter McKiernan, Christopher Vas and Peter Waring

British Library Cataloguing-in-Publication Data
A catalogue record for this book is available from the British Library

Library of Congress Cataloging-in-Publication Data
A catalog record has been requested for this book

ISBN: 978-1-138-59441-8 (hbk)
ISBN: 978-0-429-48890-0 (ebk)

Typeset in Times
by Out of House Publishing

Contents

Figures

Tables

Authors

Azad Bali is a Lecturer in Public Policy at the University of Melbourne. Prior to Melbourne, Bali taught at Murdoch University and Nanyang Technological University. His research and teaching interests lie in comparative public policy and public financial management in Asia. Some of Bali's research has been published in leading journals including *Public Policy and Administration, Social Policy and Administration,* and *Australian Journal of Public Administration* amongst others. Bali also serves on the editorial team of Policy Design & Practice.

Peter McKiernan is Professor of Management at the University of Strathclyde in Scotland. Previously, he was Dean and Sir Walter Murdoch Professor of Management at the School of Management and Governance at Murdoch University, Australia. He has been honoured with seven international Fellowships, an inaugural Companionship of the CABS, a CEEMAN Institutional Champion Award and the Richard Whipp Life Time Achievement Award of the BAM. He has published widely in top rated journals in Europe and the USA and is co-founder of both EURAM and its journal – the *European Management Review.* Together with his co-authors, he was instrumental in founding the Singapore Centre for Research in Productivity and Innovation (SCRIPT) in 2015.

Christopher Vas is Founding Director of Murdoch University's first offshore R&D Centre – Singapore Centre for Research in Innovation, Productivity and Technology (SCRIPT). With Chris's portfolio covering research, innovation and engagement he has worked closely with industry and government across Australasia. He was Executive Director and Commissioner of the Second Murdoch Commission on Food Security, Trade and Regional Partnerships. Equipped with an Executive Certificate in Strategy and Innovation from MIT Sloan School of Management, Chris is Co-Founder and Board Director of FutureSafe Tech.

Peter Waring is Murdoch University's Singapore Dean and is based in Singapore. Peter is responsible for advancing the University's academic and strategic interests in Singapore. He is Co-Founder and Chair of Murdoch's first spin out company in Singapore, FutureSafe Technologies. As a qualified lawyer, Peter also holds degrees in Commerce and Management and is a graduate of the Australian Institute of Company Directors. He is the co-author of five books on employment relations and more than 100 academic publications in total. His research and teaching interests span the business and law fields of employment relations, human resource management, corporate governance and labour law.

Acknowledgements

First, we wish to thank the Singapore Innovation and Productivity Institute (SIPI) and SPRING Singapore for their support of this research. In particular, we wish to make special mention of Mr Surajit Dhar, Ms Gillian Lim and Mr Chang Phuan Heng of the SIPI. Also, our thanks go to Mr Lam Joon Khoi (Secretary-General of the Singapore Manufacturing Federation) and Dr Michael Teng (Assistant Secretary-General of the Singapore Manufacturing Federation). We gratefully appreciate the guidance of our Chief Expert, Professor Foo Check Teck, for his constructive comments and mentorship throughout the project.

Second, we wish to acknowledge the wonderful service of our student research assistants including Ms Amrita Kaur, Mr Alvin Tan, Ms Andrina Lee, Ms Dewi Lasmini Bte Abdul Rashid, Ms Dawn Tan, Ms Felicia Xu, Mr Ellis Tan and Ms Nur Atiqa Binte Arbain; and constructive comments received from Dr Richa Sivakoti and Dr Mukul Asher.

Third, we wish to pay tribute to the many SME leaders and managers who gave up their valuable time to participate in this study. We trust that its results will be of continuing utility and relevance for them.

Fourth, we would like to show our appreciation for the research support offered by Murdoch University (Australia) and its executive team – Professors Richard Higgott, Anne Capling and David Morrison. The university's encouragement led to the setting up of its first international research centre – the Singapore Centre for Research in Innovation and Productivity (SCRIPT).

Finally, we would like to thank our publishers, Routledge, and their supportive staff, who encouraged us at each step of a long journey, Matthew Shobbrook and Hannah Ferguson. Additionally, Andrew Lowe's diligence as a text editor allowed us to progress in a professional manner.

Azad Bali
Chris Vas
Peter McKiernan
Peter Waring

1 Introduction

1.1 Project background

The engine of small and medium sized enterprise (SME) productivity is an influential driver of economic growth in advanced world economies like the USA, Germany, Japan and South Korea. As Singapore witnessed throughout the 2000s, when the engine stalls, productivity falters and a country can fall well behind its major competitors (see Table 1.1, below). In this city-state, this decline triggered a transformational policy by a government intent on forging a 'high skill–high productivity' future. Government's resolve in the relentless pursuit of improved productivity is evidenced by the 200 references to 'productivity' in its Budget statements from 2010 to 2014 compared with only 20 references in the decade up to 2010 (Au Yong, 2014).

Ironically, previously articulated reasons for Singapore's economic success included a plentiful access to relatively inexpensive foreign labour, but persistent prediction of inferior productivity growth had forced the government to take immediate action. By 2017, foreigners made up around 38% of the total active labour force of 3.7 million (Department of Statistics, 2017) – with an even greater proportion employed by SMEs. Given substantial evidence that its low productivity growth occurred in sectors where foreigners dominated the workforce (e.g., Shanmugaratnam, 2013), the foundations of recovery focused on improving productivity and innovation by limiting access to foreign workers by imposing levies and restricting work permits – signals that were heard in all sectors as warning bells for the need to improve performance. Government rhetoric acted to reinforce the message:

> Raising productivity is not just our most important economic priority but enables us to build a better society. Higher productivity is the only sustainable way to raise incomes for ordinary Singaporeans, and provide jobs that give people a sense of responsibility and empowerment.
> (T. Shanmugaratnam, Deputy Prime
> Minister and Minister of Finance, 2013, B13)

Table 1.1 Global productivity growth rates – 2012, 2013 and 2018

Regional indicators	2012	2013	2018
			PROJECTED
North America			
Labour productivity growth	0.9%	0.9%	1.5%
GDP growth	2.8%	1.9%	3.0%
Euro region			
Labour productivity growth	–0.1%	0.4%	1.4%
GDP growth	–0.07%	–0.3%	2.4%
Labour productivity growth in...			
Brazil	–0.4%	0.8%	–0.2%
China	7.3%	7.1%	4.3%
India	3.1%	2.4%	5.2%
Japan	1.2%	0.8%	0.9%
Russia	3.1%	1.6%	0.9%
Singapore	–2.5%	1.6%	2.8%
United Kingdom	–1.8%	0.5%	0.8%
United States	0.7%	0.9%	1.5%

Source: Adapted from the Conference Board's Report on Global Productivity 2013 and 2018

As Singaporean SMEs employ around 70% of all labour, this seemed an obvious place to start the search for improvements in productivity and innovation, especially in the manufacturing sector:

> We must help our SME sector revitalise itself. There are however wide divergences in efficiency amongst SMEs, even in the same industries.
> (Shanmugaratnam, 2013, C18)

Traditionally, Singapore has been regarded as an exemplar economy by experts and governments, both locally and further afield. For instance, the World Economic Forum Global Competitiveness Report (GCR) 2017/18 ranked Singapore third behind Switzerland and the United States for competitiveness. Yet, a dilemma remains between Singapore's reputation as a competitive economy and its poor record on most comparative measures of productivity and innovation. For instance, the GCR on business sophistication and technology readiness ranks Singapore at 18 and 14 respectively. While it is projected that Singapore's labour productivity in 2018 will surpass 2%, its total labour productivity grew annually by 1.6% between 2008 and 2013, marginally higher than the 1.1% pa during the previous 5 years. Although there have been advances in labour productivity, in particular sectors of the economy, a structural shift in employment away from these productive sectors

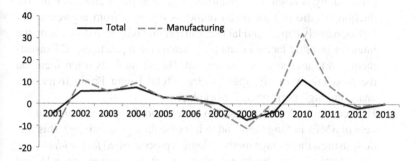

Figure 1.1 Productivity in Singapore
Source: Adapted using data from *Singapore Yearbook of Manpower Statistics* (2011); ibid. (2013)

has resulted in declining total labour productivity (Goh, 2013). Such sectoral changes are not unique to Singapore, as they are prevalent in other economies undergoing structural changes (e.g., Finland, Japan and Germany). The sharp departure from the trend in 2009/10 comes off a low base, following the decline since 2005. Total labour productivity in manufacturing has mirrored that of the whole economy over the time frame covered – a strange finding, given that the former sector has shrunk from 33% in 2000 to 25% in 2006 and accounted for less than 20% of GDP in 2014 (Figure 1.1).

1.2 Objective and aims

To explore this problematique of productivity and innovation amongst Singapore's SMEs, the government body 'Singapore Institute for Productivity and Innovation (SIPI)' commissioned a major research project during 2013–2015. This study was guided by one main objective:

> To characterise industry performance in areas of innovation and productivity through the establishment of top 5 to 8 indicators in operational performance and building a good benchmarking database of 200 local SME manufacturing and engineering companies.

To achieve this objective, the study attempted to achieve three aims:

1) What are the key drivers of Total Factor Productivity and Innovation amongst SMEs in Singapore's manufacturing sector? Drivers of TFP were identified and analysed in the country's manufacturing sector.

Productivity is often conceptualised as a measure of efficiency in production, a ratio of how much output is obtained from a given set of inputs, namely capital and labour. But, productivity also depends on the intensity of other factor inputs e.g., management practices, ICT investment, R&D intensity and innovation. Hence, analysts often focus on the productivity of all input factors – Total Factor Productivity – in analysing high-performance workplaces.

2) How can these drivers be used to understand the state of competitiveness of SMEs in Singapore and to improve their productivity? This was done using a three-stage methodological process of: a) *factor identification* informed through a review of the extant literature review, a Delphi study amongst global experts and personal interviews with CEOs; b) *factor specification* through content analysis of the triangulated output in a) above; and c) *factor verification* through primary data collection amongst a structured sample of 215 SMEs in Singapore's manufacturing sectors.

3) How can we develop a mechanism for observing the evolution of SMEs productivity and innovation? This was done by creating a Webportal, through which firms can benchmark their productivity and innovation practices with rival and non-rival firms, both within their sub-sector and across the industry. By creating a 'composite total factor productivity' score for each firm, their current position in their sector and potential future position after strategic changes can be identified.

1.3 Philosophy

In addressing this pressing competitive topic for firms, sectors and nations, our approach involved:

Interdisciplinarity – with specialist academics covering macro and micro economics, political science, industrial relations, strategic management and human resource management;

Knowledge co-production – involving the intellectual engagement of academics with mangers and government bodies;

Comprehensive – including the identification and analysis of total factors of production rather than simply capital and labour;

Rigorous method – using both primary and secondary data and triangular data gathering from a Delphi study, stratified random sample interviews from global, regional and local actors and a critique of the extant literatures;

Dynamic tool building – through the creation of a 'live' web portal, whose measures of productivity and innovation competence can assist SMEs to judge their present position and adopt strategy advice to 'improve their performance';

Policy orientation – the discovery and analysis of the total factors of production and their embodiment in a dynamic web portal enables firms, sector bodies and government to assess their competitiveness continuously.

1.4 Route-map

After this Introduction, the book is structured into five further chapters, that progress the objective and aims in a logical manner. Chapter 2 paints the broader South East Asian SME context in terms of productivity and innovation (P&I). It begins with an analysis of disaggregated time series data on economic growth and role of productivity in driving growth and development. Inevitably, this comparison triggers an argument about policy imperatives in the different countries; what seems to work and what does not. The chapter content allows the reader to compare the performance of countries with each other and allows them to question the effectiveness of a country's policy. In addition, it introduces many Western readers to the lesser known economies of South East Asia and their relative performances. In particular, the reader is introduced to perhaps the most dynamic of these economies – Singapore. The narrative shows how this city-state has managed P&I in the SME sector and identifies the current problems that it faces.

Chapter 3 introduces the reader to the method deployed in the research project that provided the primary evidence for the investigation of P&I in Singaporean SMEs. The methodology is explained as a three-part process including the systematic literature survey above, which involved reviews of academic databases like Scopus, Google and the Web of Science. This was followed by a series of interviews (20) with the CEOs of Singaporean SMEs to surface the policy context and the practical challenges that they face. Finally, a Delphi study of global and local experts and thought leaders (including academics, government officials and policy makers) was conducted and focused on the drivers of P&I in SMEs. The triangulated approach produced six thematic drivers of total factor productivity: technology and capital utilisation; pay and performance management; training, development and organisational learning; innovation culture, government policy, markets and regulation; and leadership and management quality.

Chapter 4 outlines the research findings for the reader. It begins with an array of descriptive statistics that cover performance, employment, productivity, ownership and operational indicators. Then, the results of the six drivers of total factor productivity (TFP) are examined in sequence with a comprehensive graphical display and a detailed narrative discussion. The reader is presented with a series of arguments around the positive aspects of P&I practice in Singaporean SMEs and, most important, around those aspects of failure or under-performance that attract immediate policy recommendations. These include a lack of advanced production technologies e.g., robotics and computer numerically controlled (CNC) machinery, restricted benchmarking activity, low skill levels, lack of incentives for innovative solutions, sticky career progression, little employee training or management development, low investment in R&D, and a heavy reliance on foreign labour. The chapter concludes by illustrating how a composite index of SME performance on its productivity and innovation practices is developed from the six drivers to form a composite index for each firm as an input into a dynamic web portal. Composite scores are developed for each sub-sector in Singapore's manufacturing sector. In Singapore, the research shows that the pharmaceuticals sector is the highest performing one, while fabricated metals and machinery and equipment (both of which contribute a large share of Singapore's manufacturing output) have relatively low composite scores. Then, the reader is shown how the six drivers of TFP vary across each sector of manufacturing e.g., computer and electronics, food and beverage and pharmaceuticals having the highest levels of innovative culture, while technology and capital utilisation is lowest in food and beverage, machinery and equipment and chemicals. This data informs the policy recommendations to government, specific to each firm's composite score.

Chapter 5 conjectures upon the policy options and practical advice as a consequence of the research findings. These support the role that the Singapore Government can play in driving future productivity in SMEs and the strategic and tactical actions that SME owners might pursue. The policy and practical advice are centred on the six key drivers of total factor productivity. Policy advice includes a lowering of the bureaucratic access barriers to available technological funding schemes; the creation of firm incentives that do not lead to 'dependency' on corporate welfare; the spread of new technology and innovations through the formation of hi-tech precincts and the co-location of firms in the same value chain; incentives for firms to create inclusive and collaborative workplaces; for the State to serve as a role model employer for high performance workplaces and to lead cultural change to innovation through a cocktail of incentives; maintain a collaborative approach of tri-partism between unions, employers and government; and the establishment of leadership training institutes and tax incentives for training.

The practical advice for SME owners includes: work with external stakeholders to follow the latest technological best practice; move into advanced manufacturing automation and cloud computing; link pay and performance management to high performance work systems; create both monetary and non-monetary incentives; ensure regular workforce training and development to help build a culture of firm-based learning; encourage continuous innovation amongst employees; empower employees to take action; engage with the plethora of government incentive schemes through discussions with SPRING; cluster and collaborate with other SME leaders; and foster personal leadership development plans.

Chapter 6 concludes the study with a recap of the objectives and aims and a summary of the research method and results, followed by a discussion of the limitations of the research. It progresses by examining the design of a performance portal, developed for SPRING as part of the research project. This tool helps SME leaders to audit their current innovation and productivity efforts and identify these with established profiles on the portal. These profiles are at different levels of technological advancement and, after identifying their current position, firms can receive advice on how to move up to the next level of sophistication. The portal is a dynamic tool and can be updated constantly as new technologies become available. Finally, the chapter moves into prospective mode by imagining the 'future of work' as noted by global experts and situates Singaporean SMEs within the imagined context. This action forces both government and SME leaders to keep their eyes on the international horizon for the arrival of tomorrow's innovation and productivity schema.

References

Au Yong, Hawyee (2014) *Singapore's Productivity Challenge: Part III.* Case Study published by the LKY School of Public Policy, National University of Singapore.

Goh, Tee Wei (2013) *A Shift-share analysis of Singapore's Labour Productivity Growth, 1998–2013*, Economic Survey of Singapore 2013, pp. 70–77.

Department of Statistics, Government of Singapore (2017) *Singapore Yearbook of Statistics.* Available at: www.singstat.gov.sg/publications/reference/yearbook-of-statistics-singapore

Ministry of Manpower (2011) *Yearbook of Manpower Statistics 2011.* Available at: www.mom.gov.sg/newsroom/press-releases/2011/report-on-wages-in-singapore-2010-and-singapore-yearbook-of-manpower-statistics-2011

Shanmugaratnam, T. (2013) *A Better Singapore: Quality Growth, An Inclusive Society*, FY 2013 Budget Statement. Available at: www.singaporebudget.gov.sg/budget_2013/budget_speech.html

World Economic Forum (2017) *The Global Competitiveness Report (2017–2018)*, September 2017: World Economic Forum. Available at: www.weforum.org/reports/the-global-competitiveness-report-2017-201

2 Economic growth and productivity in Singapore and South East Asia

This chapter provides an overview of the broad drivers of economic growth in South East Asian economies and records their actual performance from 1990 to 2017. There is an emphasis on Singapore – the region's most prosperous society that explains the key tenets of the city-state's growth and development strategy, which underpinned its economic success. Despite its economic prosperity, the chapter reveals how Singapore suffered from low productivity growth largely from pursuing a growth and development strategy which emphasised using relatively unskilled and cheap foreign labour. The government was keen to act and introduced a number of crucial reforms aimed at stemming the tide and placing SME performance on a new trajectory.

2.1 Economic trends in South East Asia

2.1.1 Regional macroeconomic comparison

In 2017, the global economy grew at 3.8% (0.5% higher than in 2016). It is expected to grow at 3.9% in 2018 and 2019. Buttressed by rising commodity prices, investments in advanced economics, growth in private consumption in emerging economies, and an uptake in world trade volume, global real GDP growth in 2017 was the strongest since 2011. Emerging and Developing Asia, including China, India, and the ASEAN-5 (Indonesia, Malaysia, Philippines, Thailand, Vietnam) – was the fastest growing region globally (International Monetary Fund, 2018), expanding its economic output by 6.5%. Table 2.1 illustrates the individual GDP and GDP per capita growth rates since 1985 for the major economies in the ASEAN region.

Against the backdrop of robust economic growth, policy makers in the region have expressed concern over the need to improve the contribution of *productivity* to economic growth. The challenge of improving productivity is not restricted to developing economies in ASEAN but, within this group,

Table 2.1 Selected economic indicators

| | GDP (Current USD bn.) | | | GDP per capita (current USD) | | | Per capita growth rates | |
	1985	2005	2015	1985	2005	2015	1985–2005	2006–2016
Indonesia	90.8	215.2	861.3	550.3	1342.5	3336.1	3.0	4.2
Malaysia	31.2	88.7	296.4	2000.1	5593.8	9648.6	3.6	3.0
Philippines	30.7	74.1	292.8	565.8	1194.7	2878.3	0.9	3.9
Singapore	19.1	87.9	296.8	6995.1	29869.9	53629.7	4.4	2.6
Thailand	38.9	169.3	399.2	747.5	2893.7	5814.9	4.9	2.9
Vietnam	14.1	20.7	193.2	230.9	683.6	2065.2	4.8	5.0

Source: World Bank (2018)

even Singapore – the most prosperous economy in ASEAN – had much work to do, after years of low productivity growth.

Most growth accounting studies use a neoclassical framework. Which disaggregates the contribution of various inputs (labour and capital) and total factor productivity (TFP) in economic growth (Barro, 1996; Chen, 1997). The capital input consists of both the information and communication technology (ICT) and non-ICT capital. The labour input reflects both the quantity of hours worked, as well as labour quality – this captures human capital accumulation. Such approaches usually measure TFP residually, which accounts for the contribution of technical progress and other unobservable factors. One of the most recent studies of the determinants of economic growth in developing Asia is by Vu Minh Khuong, whose main results for South East Asia are summarised in this chapter (Vu, 2014), and extended using more recently published data from the Conference Board's Total Economy Dataset.

The economies of Singapore, Hong Kong, South Korea and Taiwan – popularly known as the Asian Tigers – grew between 3.9% (Hong Kong) and 6.5% (Singapore) between 1990 and 2010. While non-ICT capital accounted for most of the capital inputs across all four economies, the shares were relatively higher for Hong Kong and Singapore. Similarly, South Korea and Taiwan experienced higher contributions of labour quality in total labour inputs than either Hong Kong or Singapore. Consequently, the share of TFP to economic growth – a proxy for technology and economic efficiency – was much higher in South Korea and Taiwan. For instance, the contribution of TFP to economic growth between 1990 and 2010 was 7.7% in Singapore; 42.9% in Hong Kong; and 49.2% in South Korea (Vu, 2013: 147).

The ASEAN-5 economies grew between 3.8% (Philippines) and 7.2% (Vietnam) during the 1990–2010 period. Capital inputs (mostly non-ICT capital) accounted for between 45% (Malaysia) and 69% (Indonesia) of economic growth experienced in the region (Vu, 2013). Similar to Singapore and Hong Kong, the contribution of quality labour to total labour inputs was relatively low. The only exception was Thailand, where quality labour accounted for about a third of total labour inputs. During the same period, the total contribution of labour inputs to economic growth was higher than that of TFP – which ranged between 8% (Indonesia) and 23% (Malaysia). Figure 2.1 illustrates growth in total factor productivity between 2000 and 2016 for ASEAN-6 economies.

Country-data (Figures 2.2–2.7) suggests large variations in the contribution of labour, capital and TFP to economic growth across the ASEAN-6 economies. The Philippines and Thailand . stand at one end of the spectrum, where TFP has contributed positively across most of the years. Indeed, Indonesia, the Philippines and Thailand – and to a lesser extent

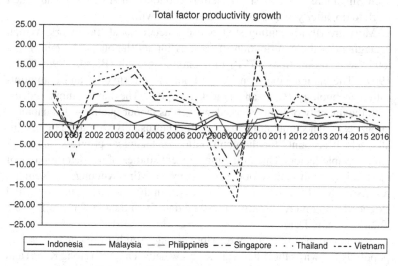

Figure 2.1 Total factor productivity growth in ASEAN-6
Source: Conference Board (2018)

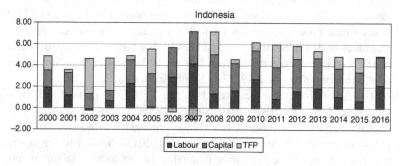

Figure 2.2 Contribution to economic growth: Indonesia
Source: Conference Board (2018)

Vietnam – have experienced positive contributions to TFP, post the major global economic decline of 2008.

2.1.2 Global competitiveness comparison

The global competitiveness index is a weighted index of 12 economic 'pillars' – institutions, infrastructure, macroeconomic environment, health

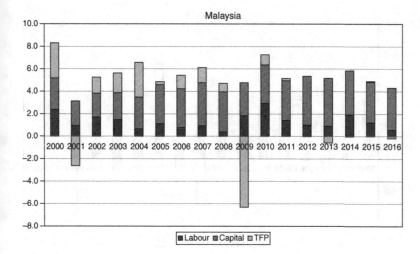

Figure 2.3 Contribution to economic growth: Malaysia
Source: Conference Board (2018)

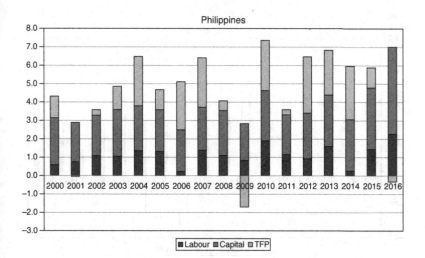

Figure 2.4 Contribution to economic growth: Philippines
Source: Conference Board (2018)

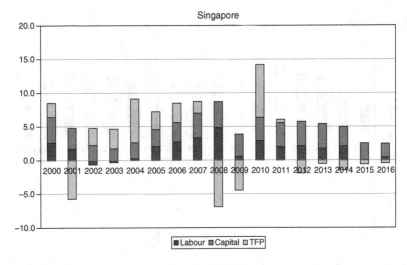

Figure 2.5 Contribution to economic growth: Singapore
Source: Conference Board (2018)

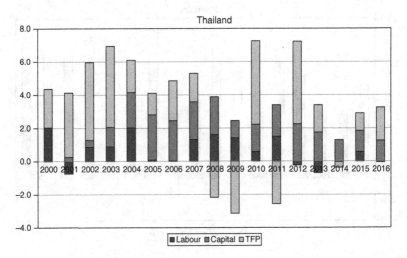

Figure 2.6 Contribution to economic growth: Thailand
Source: Conference Board (2018)

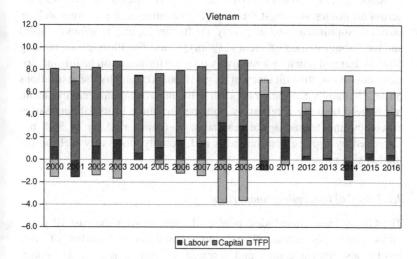

Figure 2.7 Contribution to economic growth: Vietnam
Source: Conference Board (2018)

Table 2.2 Performance across ASEAN6 on competitiveness and innovation indices

Country	Global Competitiveness Index	Global Innovation Index	Network Readiness Index	Ease of doing business
Indonesia	36 (4)	87 (6)	73 (4)	72 (5)
Malaysia	23 (2)	37 (2)	31 (2)	24 (2)
Philippines	56 (6)	73 (5)	77 (5)	113 (6)
Singapore	3 (1)	7 (1)	1 (1)	2 (1)
Thailand	32 (3)	51 (4)	62 (3)	26 (3)
Vietnam	55 (5)	47 (3)	79 (6)	68 (4)

Source: Based on official reports
Note: Numbers in parenthesis refer to a country's relative rank within the table.

and primary education, higher education and training, goods market efficiency, labour market efficiency, financial market development, technological readiness, market size, business sophistication, and innovation. Singapore ranks the highest amongst the ASEAN-6 economies, and features in the top-10 in seven of these 'pillars'. The city-state ranks first worldwide for public sector performance, while Malaysia ranks between 20 and 30 on all the pillars, except 'primary education and health', where it ranks in the mid-40s.

Ranking 36th, Indonesia has experienced improved performance across all pillars. Amongst the emerging economies, it performs well on business sophistication but poorly on 'technological readiness' (80th) and the 'labour market efficiency' (96th) pillars. The Philippines, ranking 56th, is dragged down by a relatively poor performance on health and primary education, the efficiency of its goods market, and by the institutions pillar. Thailand's economy ranks 9th in the macroeconomic environment, but is held back by a relatively poor performance in its labour market efficiency and technological readiness. Vietnam's ranking of 55th has improved by 5 places on the index and, notably, does very well on the market size pillar.

2.1.3 Global innovation comparison

The Global Innovation Index, published annually over the past 10 years, ranks economies across 81 indicators based on the quality of their institutions, human capital and research, infrastructure, market sophistication, business sophistication, knowledge and technology outputs, and creative outputs. The report highlights the growing economic dynamism in Indonesia, Philippines, Thailand and Vietnam, buttressed by participation in global value chains. The stark difference in rankings between Singapore and other economies is attributed to a larger gap in output indicators (e.g. patents, quality of scientific publications, ICT services export, etc.) rather than input indicators (expenditure on education, state of cluster development, ICT use, FDIs, knowledge-intensive employment, etc.). Singapore is the top performer in the selected innovation outputs, with two exceptions: ICT services exports, where the Philippines leads ASEAN; and trademarks by origin, where Vietnam leads ASEAN. Malaysia has the second highest scores in patents by origin, scientific and technical articles, and ICT services exports. Thailand's strengths are in citable documents and trademarks by origin, where it places 2nd.

2.1.4 Future-proof production comparison

The World Economic Forum, Future of Production Report published in 2018 ranks economies for their 'readiness' to capitalise on future production opportunities (rather than current production performance), mitigate risks and challenges, and for their resilience and agility in responding to unknown future shocks. South East Asia accounts for 5% of global manufacturing activity and three-fifths of its activity is concentrated in just five sectors: food and beverage, chemicals and chemical products, electronics, motor vehicles, and rubber and plastic products.

The range of positions across these indices reflects the heterogeneous region. Not only do these economies have large variations in economic development (Table 2.1), but also in their state capacities, and integration with global value chains. In the global and regional comparisons above, Singapore paints a picture of an exceptional economy, especially in GDP growth terms. But, this apparent success shields an underlying problem with productivity and high value-added growth, especially as this relates to productivity and innovation. The root cause appears to be an over reliance on foreign labour, especially in SMEs. The government was to take radical steps to resolve the issue.

2.2 Singapore's growth and development strategy

2.2.1 Background to economic success

Singapore has achieved remarkable economic success, multiplying its GDP manifold since the city-state achieved independence in 1965 (World Bank, 2018). Except for short recessions in 1973/74, 1985/86, 1997/98 and 2008/09, Singapore has enjoyed full employment during this period (Pang and Lim, 2015). Analysts have attributed this economic success, in part, to Singapore's long-serving regime being able to successfully pursue a 'location-based' growth strategy, which emphasises capital accumulation, attracting foreign firms (Multi National Companies – MNCs in particular), and portfolio investors (Asher, Bali and Kwan, 2015; Lim, 2016; Low and Vadaketh, 2014). Due to falling fertility rates and rising longevity, Singapore's location-based growth strategy has required a substantial inflow of foreign labour, and a relatively inflexible age at which individuals decide to exit the labour force.[1] At the end of 2016, Singapore citizens comprised 60.7% of the total population, with permanent residents comprising 9.4% (Department of Statistics, 2017). Thirty-eight percent of Singapore's labour force (of 3.7 million at end 2017) were non-residents. The inflow of foreign labour has been beneficial to Singapore in economic and fiscal terms but, equally, as Low and Vadaketh (2014) document, has posed many challenges which are discussed later in this chapter.

Tan and Bhaskaran (2016) summarise three elements of the Singapore Government's approach to economic management. First, a strong belief that the government plays a key role in the economy. This includes public investments through government-owned or government-linked and managed corporations (GLCs), not only in strategic areas such as infrastructure, telecommunication, shipping, and aviation, but in areas of service delivery including water, waste management, and commercial banking. The sustained dominance of the public sector in a relatively small and open economy may have contributed to the 'crowding out' of private investment in product and factor markets (Pang and Lim, 2016:156). Further, through GLCs and sovereign wealth funds, Singapore participates in business and economic activities across the globe. The second element is the unfettered pursuit of, and the primacy of, economic growth. This has required remaining economically competitive and attractive to international businesses and capital. The Singapore government has been extremely successful in lowering the costs of doing business, as is evidenced by its rankings in Table 2.2.

Asher et al. (2015) have argued that sustaining such an approach has resulted in a much larger share of capital in national income than wages. For instance, the share of labour income averaged 42% between 2015 and 2017, with the corresponding capital share at 52% (Ministry of Trade and Industry, 2017). Taxes on capital income have been substantially reduced in the past two decades and, as of mid-2018, there was no income tax on interest income, dividends, most capital gains, and foreign-earned income. A tax system in which capital income, accounting for more than 50% of national income and accruing disproportionately to the upper deciles of the population, is taxed lightly contributes to and perpetuates inequalities in a society (Asher et al., 2015). For instance, between 2010 and 2016 the GINI coefficient[2] – which measures the statistical dispersion of wealth – varied between 0.458 and 0.478, and 0.402 and 0.425, after accounting for government transfers and taxes (Department of Statistics, 2017: Table 2.3). The real median wages of Singaporean citizens and PRs in the lower half of the income distribution had stagnated over the 15-year period ending in 2012, while that of the top most quintile increased by 46% (Hui and Toh, 2014). In addition, Singapore has maintained a narrow tax base, with only about half of the labour force paying income tax (Department of Statistics, 2017).[3]

The third element of Singapore's approach to economic management, Tan and Bhaskaran (2016) claim, is the capacity of the State to mobilise resources to meet its economic objectives. This has been aided by decades of political stability and a significant presence in the economy by direct participation, state-led planning and the use of interventionist policies (Lim, 2016).

2.2.2 Fiscal perspectives on Singapore's growth strategy

A defining feature of the Singapore economy is that its approach to managing its public finances, and public expenditure programmes, is consistent with its growth strategy. Asher et al. (2015) and Kwan et al. (2016) present evidence to show how relatively low levels of public expenditure and sustained economic growth have resulted in structural budgetary surpluses. Asher et al. (2015) argue that these surpluses were necessary to instill investor confidence, as well as manage expectations of macroeconomic stability. They estimate that the tax revenue to GDP ratio has remained relatively constant at around 13% over the past 15 years. Over the same period, the share of total government revenue to GDP peaked at 24% in 2007 and plateaued at 18% in 2009. This suggests there may have been a shift away from relying on taxation as the main revenue instrument; instead, non-tax revenue, including unconventional sources,[4] has become more prominent. Total expenditure peaked at 17.7% of GDP in 2005 and fell below 15% between 2006 and 2013.

2.2.3 The problem of productivity

Singapore's productivity problem is not new. As early as 1961, The Winsemius Report on Industrialization on Singapore highlighted that:

> Singapore's manufacturing industry can be divided into two groups. On the one side, there are a limited number of usually well managed factories, for the greater part subsidiaries of foreign firms. On the other side, there exist many small establishments characterized by low productivity.
>
> (as cited in Au Yong, 2014a:6)

Several studies found that productivity in the manufacturing sector in Singapore in the 1970s was extremely low (Tsao, 1985). Yuan Tsao (1985) in an aptly titled essay, *Growth without productivity: Singapore manufacturing in the 1970s*, attributed this to: a) the pursuit and dominance of foreign capital; b) the reliance on relatively low-cost and low-skilled foreign labour; and c) systemic lack of industrial acumen. Paul Krugman famously compared Singapore's economic performance to that of the Soviet Union and argued that most of its growth stemmed from factor accumulation rather than harnessing economic efficiencies (Krugman, 1994:64–66).

Pang and Lim (2016:149–155) document the restructuring reforms implemented in Singapore in the late 1970s in response to the recognition of low productivity growth. These include attracting foreign direct investments, 'high-value added industry' clusters including biomedical, chemicals, aerospace and precision engineering. While these reforms continued to contribute to Singapore's economic prosperity, they did little to add to Singapore's productivity growth (Figure 1.1).

The average labour productivity growth has trended downwards since 1975, even despite the upward trend during 1985–1996 (Vu, 2014: 10); and productivity growth has been lowest in sectors with a high dependence on low-skilled foreign labour (Shanmugaratnam, 2013).[5] Pang and Lim (2016:151) cite a discussion paper by K. Nomura and T. Amano which estimates that TFP contributed negatively to economic growth from 1974–1980 and in the 1980s and 1990s; from 1974–2011 capital inputs contributed to about three-fifths of economic growth, and capital deepening accounted for nearly four-fifths of observed labour productivity (see Figure 1.1).

In a series of well-developed case studies, Au Yong (2014a; 2014b; 2014c; 2014d) claims that Singapore's challenges of productivity are a direct consequence of its growth model, and its reliance on both MNCs and a relatively cheap supply of foreign labour. It is not that policy makers were unaware of the perils of low productivity growth. For instance, Richard Hu, the Finance Minister, in his Budget Statement in 1998 remarked:

> We have therefore been using a pool of foreign workers as a buffer to cope with business cycles and economic fluctuations. However, we must not lose sight of the social and economic costs of an increasing dependence on foreign workers.
>
> (as cited in Au Yong 2014b:9)

However, Singapore's growth strategy has been shaped by social and political constraints that the Singapore government faced. For instance, as the subsequent section will argue, at critical junctures policy makers were acutely aware of the challenges of foreign labour. However, they were unable to reduce the growing dependence on foreign labour as many SMEs derived their economic competitiveness by using cheap and relatively unskilled foreign labour. Pang and Lim (2016:152) and Au Yong (2014a) show how at various critical junctures, plans to reduce the dependence were scuttled in response to exogenous shocks such as economic recessions or in response to pressures from the SME leaders. Even as recent as 2017, increases in foreign worker levies introduced across all industrial sub-sectors were deferred for sectors affected by 'cyclical weaknesses' such as the marine and process sectors (Today Online, 2017).[6]

2.3 Singapore's reliance on foreign labour

2.3.1 The historical context

To understand Singapore's dependency on foreign labour, particularly in SMEs, and the concomitant challenges this has created, it is necessary to view temporary migrant labour in its full historical context. At various times throughout its history, the authorities in Singapore have relaxed or tightened the flow of foreign labour to suit economic, social and political circumstances. As Pang and Lim (1982: 548; 2015) have observed, the Singapore economy was 'founded' on migrant labour, and contemporary Singaporeans are the descendants of the Chinese diaspora of the southern coastal regions of China, as well as indentured labour from the subcontinent, the Malaysian peninsula and the Indonesian archipelago. The Chinese immigrant population was by far the largest, attracted by the rubber boom of the early twentieth century (Pang and Lim, 1982 : 549). These inward flows of migrant labour supported the economic interests of the British colonial authorities, who encouraged immigration largely without restriction until the surrender of the city to General Yamashita of the Japanese Imperial Army. Following the cessation of hostilities in 1945, the Colonial authorities imposed an Immigration Ordinance to restrict 'the number and quality of immigrants to Singapore' (Pang and Lim, 1982).

In 1965, Singapore, somewhat reluctantly, became an independent republic after being unceremoniously ousted from the Federation of Malaya. Many doubted Singapore's ability to survive this tumultuous period. Indeed, it had very few of the basic elements needed to sustain its sovereignty. There was no permanent water supply, no substantial agricultural sector, nor plentiful mineral resources. Singapore had a diverse population with racial tension; an under equipped and untrained set of armed forces, and a narrow economic base. Despite these challenges (or perhaps because of them), Singapore's leadership drove a rapid industrialisation agenda, underpinned by rivers of foreign capital. Significant labour shortages in the late 1960s and 1970s, led to a relaxing of policy to enable the extensive use of foreign temporary labour in all sectors of the economy. In the late 1970s, the State implemented a 'corrective high wage' policy designed at reducing the migrant worker dependency. However, as Pang and Lim (1982: 550) noted, this exacerbated the tight labour market leading to production delays. By 1981, the government had to liberalise foreign worker rules, in response to industry concerns. However, as the State understood the consequences of such liberalisation on productivity, it cautioned employers to regard freely-available migrant labour as a temporary measure only. The then Prime Minister, Lee Kuan Yew, was reported in the Straits Times as stating that Singapore's manufacturers would need to '*mechanize, automate, computerize and improve management to cut down on workers or they will have to relocate their factories*' (cited in Pang and Lim, 1982: 552). Policy makers were aware of the socio-economic challenges of this reliance on foreign labour. Former Prime Minister Goh Chok Tong, speaking in 1979, cautioned that a high dependence on migrant workers was economically undesirable as:

> It helps to sustain low-skilled, low productivity and labour-intensive industries. These industries in turn can afford to pay only low wages which in turn, cause them to depend on more imported labour to keep their wage costs down.
>
> (Cited in Au Yong, 2014a)

The Minister of Labour, S. Jaykumar, echoed this refrain, and emphasised that migrant workers were not a permanent solution to addressing Singapore's labour market *challenges:*

> What every Singaporean needs to know is that there is a large number of foreign workers, 150,000, and we have to have them temporarily. But in the long-term economic and social interest, they will have to be phased out.[7]

Similarly, the then Finance Minister, Tony Tan, who later served as President of the Republic between 2011 and 2017, stressed that:

> [a] solution to our labour shortage cannot be an indefinite and ever-growing dependence on foreign workers. The experience of countries that have indiscriminately allowed large numbers of foreign workers to settle permanently shows that this gives rise to social and political problems of such magnitudes as to threaten the cohesiveness and sta-bility of their societies.
>
> (Cited in Pang and Lim, 2015:141)

This clear advice was not adopted wholly by manufacturers and other employers in Singapore, as they continued to employ large numbers of for-eign workers. The total number of non-residents in the labour market grew from 20,710 in 1970 to 79,275 in 1980. Part of this is attributed to strong growth in employment in the manufacturing sector, which expanded by 350% between 1967 and 1973 (Yap and Gee, 2016: 202). The economic recession in 1985 further incentivised businesses – especially SMEs – to lower labour costs. The government also removed the statutory requirement for foreigners (and those employing them) to make mandatory contributions to the Central Provident Fund (an implicit tax on wage income) (Au Yong, 2014b:10). In turn, this lowered the costs of hiring foreign workers.

In 1987, the Singapore Government introduced monthly levies paid by employers on each foreign worker they employed, as well as a 'dependency

Table 2.3 Singapore population size and growth

Year	Total population	Resident population***	Total labour force	Foreign labour force	Foreign share of total labour force
1970	2,074.50	2,013.60	723.00	83.10	11.50
1980	2,413.90	2,282.10	1,093.00	79.80	7.30
1990	3,047.10	2,735.90	1,673.70	300.80	18.0*
2000	4,027.90	3,273.40	2,330.50	686.20	29.40**
2010	5,076.70	3,771.70	3,135.90	1,088.60	34.70
2016	5,607.30	3,933.60	3,672.80	1,415.20	38.50

Source: Yap and Gee (2016: Tables 1 and 3) and Department of Statistics (2017)

Note: *Data for 1991; **Data for 2001; *** Total Labour Force includes citizens, permanent residents and foreigners. Resident includes citizens and permanent residents.

ceiling' to limit the ratio of foreign workers in any employer's work-force (Athukorala and Manning, 1999). Despite these increasing costs and restrictions, the foreign workforce continued to swell. By 1990, it had grown to 248,000, and onwards to 670,000 by 2006 (Yeoh, 2007). In response to the Asian Financial Crisis in 1997, and to reduce the impact on businesses and employment levels, the government reduced the contribution of employers to an individual's provident fund.[8] These cuts, similar to those made during the previous recession in 1985, reduced employer's contributions to 10%. In the following years, the government emphasised investments in research and development, and improving capabilities rather than lowering costs. While the Singapore economy improved its manufacturing capabilities and moved up the value chain, its reliance on foreign labour continues. By 2016, the foreign labour force more than doubled and was 38% of the total labour force (Table 2.3).

2.3.2 The modern labour context and its emergent social problems

At the end of 2016, the total resident labour force stood at 2.32 million people (62% of the total labour force) while foreigners made up the balance (Table 2.3). The proportion of foreigners in employment has grown steadily from 11.5% in 1970 to more than a third in recent years. This large share of foreign labour became a significant political issue for the government during the 2011 General Elections (Low and Vadaketh, 2014). Both Singapore's strong economy and its low birth rate – which at just 1.1 lies below the fertility rate of Japan – have been responsible for attracting such a foreign presence. Unlike Japan though, Singapore has shown little hesitation in importing foreign temporary labour to supplement the residential workforce in various industries, occupations and skill levels. As Table 2.4 highlights, the single largest employer of foreign labour is the construction industry. In 2017, it employed nearly 26% of the total foreign labour pool. These workers are typically employed through recruitment agencies and come from low wage developing countries in the region, such as Bangladesh, India, China and Indonesia. Other work permit holders (visa for unskilled or semi-skilled foreign workers) work as cleaners, or in marine and offshore engineering, road maintenance, manufacturing and in other industries where local workers are not found frequently. A significant number (246,800) of foreign workers are female domestic workers from countries such as the Philippines, Indonesia and Myanmar. Table 2.4 outlines the type of employment permits, workforce numbers and who they relate to in Singapore, as of December 2017.

In Singapore, the foreign workers who mostly experience relatively poor working conditions and precarious employment arrangements are those on temporary work permits, as opposed to expatriate professionals and executives, who are sponsored by a home-country corporation and who tend to enjoy superior wages and benefits (Ang, Van Dyne and Begley, 2003). It is the former category that is recruited by agencies from developing countries in the region to take on low wage jobs in Singapore. Although their employment is regulated by the Employment Act 1968 (aside from foreign domestic workers), wages are not otherwise regulated and are not normally eligible for promotion, training and development opportunities, paid vacations, pension or superannuation payments. Their low bargaining power is compounded by language and cultural barriers, as well as their dependence on their employer for accommodation while in Singapore. Indeed, there have been many reported cases where employers have been convicted for offences relating to accommodation of their foreign workers.

For instance, between January and December 2008, the Ministry of Manpower found that 42% of the 661 inspected premises were overcrowded and posed public health and fire safety concerns. Consequently, 1370 foreign workers had to be relocated, and enforcement actions were carried out against 1052 employers for not providing acceptable accommodation for the foreign workers (Ministry of Manpower, 2008). In one such egregious case in March 2012, the Ministry of Manpower successfully prosecuted two managers for making false declarations as to the residential address of their foreign workers, when the workers were forced to live in rubbish bin centres (Ministry of Manpower, 2012). In many cases, employers circumvent housing guidelines and make foreign workers live in illegally converted dormitories, that pose significant health and safety risks (Ministry of Manpower, 2011). In 2016, two companies were convicted and fined for

Table 2.4 Pass (Visa) types, workforce numbers and types of employment in Singapore

Foreign workforce numbers				
Pass (visa) type	As at end December 2017	As share of total foreign work force (%)	As share of total labour force (%)	Explanation
Employment Pass (EP)	187,700	13.7	5.1	This visa is for skilled professionals and executives who earn a monthly income over at least S$3600
S Pass	184,000	13.4	5.0	Largely for diploma holders and those with a technical skill base an a monthly income over at least S$200
Work permit (total)	965,000	70.5	26.2	Work permits for unskilled/semi-skilled foreign workers
Work permit (foreign domestic worker)	246,800			Mostly female domestic workers
Work permit (construction)	284,900			Mostly for male foreign workers employed in the construction sector
Other work passes	30,700			Includes holders of training work permits
Total foreign workforce	1,368,200	1.00	37.3	

Source: Adapted from Ministry of Manpower (2018)

failing to provide accurate information to the authorities on the accommodation of their foreign workers, and for poor and unsafe living conditions of 41 foreign workers between 2012 and 2014 (Ministry of Manpower, 2016). If foreign workers join registered trade unions, they can enjoy the benefits of workplace representation, legal aid and participation in collective bargaining. However, low salaries and the transient nature of foreign workers mitigate higher union density levels, which results in lower collective bargaining coverage than for the local labour force. According to the NTUC, in 2010, approximately 15% (84,000) of their 560,000 strong members were foreign workers. This represents just over 9% of all foreign workers on temporary work permits.

2.3.3 The productivity policy remedy

In the context of achieving sustained productivity growth, much effort has been directed towards the foreign labour issue. In May 2009, at the depths of the global financial crisis and at a time of economic contraction in Singapore, Prime Minister Lee Hsien Loong established the Economic Strategies Committee (ESC), with members drawn from the private sector, labour movement and academia. The Committee's purpose was to:

> develop strategies for Singapore to maximize our opportunities in a new world environment by building our capabilities and making the best use of our resources with the aim of achieving sustained and inclusive growth,
>
> (ESC, 2010)

In its final report published in 2010, the ESC called for 'productivity-driven growth' and took a rationalist tone, arguing that:

> ...we must allow market forces to restructure our economy providing more room for efficient enterprises to grow and pushing less efficient activities either to upgrade or phase out.
>
> (ESC, 2010, ii)

In a section entitled 'Managing our Foreign Worker Dependence', the report notes that:

> ...we cannot increase the number of foreign workers as liberally as we did over the last decade or else we will run up against real physical and social limits.
>
> (p. 18)

According to the report, the solution was to rely upon the 'price mechanism' and raise foreign worker levies gradually, to give firms time to adjust and invest in productivity (p. 18). The ESC's reference to 'social limits' proved prescient of the issues that would become heated during what is often regarded as the watershed 2011 General Election.

At the May 2011 General Election, the main opposition Workers Party actively campaigned regarding the role of foreign workers in the Singapore workforce and in doing so, tapped into a concern that foreign workers both reduce employment opportunities for citizens and place additional stress on Singapore's stretched infrastructure and housing. Singapore's founding Prime Minister, and then Minister Mentor, remarked in a speech in 2011 that 'We've grown in the last five years by just importing labour. Now, the people feel uncomfortable, there are too many foreigners.' These concerns also intersect with observations that Singapore's faltering productivity was a direct consequence of this growth in low-cost foreign labour (Pang and Lim, 2015). The Workers' Party's aggressive campaigning on this, and other salient issues, saw it win six seats from the People's Action Party, in an election where the ruling party's vote fell to its lowest level since independence. As a consequence, following the election, the Ministry of Manpower implemented several measures to restrict the growth in the size of the foreign labour force. These measures included raising the cost of foreign worker levies paid by employers and changing the qualifying salary criteria for Employment Pass and S Pass holders.

The Ministry of Manpower (2015: 2) observed that because of measures to restrict the use of foreign labour, the growth in the non-resident labour force had fallen from 11.2% per annum between 2004 and 2009 to 5.2% per annum from 2009 to 2014. The capacity of Singaporean employers to attract and deploy foreign workers at relatively low cost is a significant source of flexibility and a large part of the explanation as to why non-standard employment arrangements amongst Singaporean citizens are low by international standards. In 2010, just 9.7% of Singaporeans were engaged in part-time employment compared to an OECD average of 16.6%, and those of Australia (24.9%), the UK (24.6%) and Germany (21.7%) – (OECD, 2011).

Clearly, the government has placed renewed emphasis on improving productivity growth. In addition, it has acknowledged that the sectors which were most dependent on foreign workers are the ones that are the furthest behind international standards of productivity (Shanmugaratnam, 2013). The recalibrated growth strategy aims to reduce the reliance on foreign labour, revive manufacturing growth, and make productivity the cornerstone of Singapore's economic reforms. The Government's latest resolve to improve productivity can perhaps be best captured by the Finance Minister's remarks during the Budget Speech in 2014:

Box 2.1:   Financial incentives and grants available to SMEs

STP – SMEs Talent Program – provides for funding to recruit fresh graduates from vocational institutes up to 70% of pay for 2 years (and includes training and education support).

ICV – Innovation and Capability Vouchers – up to 8 vouchers (each of $5000) to improve capabilities in productivity, HRM, financial management and innovation.

iSPRINT – Increase SME Productivity with Infocomm Adoption and Transformation – 70% of expenses to improve (ceiling at $2000) and transform ($20,000) business practices.

IPG – ICT for Productivity and Growth – matching funding for using wireless and monthly subscription equipment.

PIC – Productivity and Innovation Credit – 60% cash rebate or 400% tax rebate on up to S$100,000 on 6 areas: IT and automation, R&D, Training, buying IPRs, registering IPRs, and approved design projects

WCS – Wage Credit Scheme – pays for 40% of annual wage increments for qualified SME employees who earn a gross wage of S$4000.0 or below

Other schemes: Enhanced Training, Work Pro, Market Readiness Assistance Grant, Micro Loan Programme, Double Taxation Deduction, ACE Start up grants

---

> Raising productivity is not just our most important economic priority but enables us to build a better society. Higher productivity is the only sustainable way to raise incomes for ordinary Singaporeans and provide jobs that give people a sense of responsibility and empowerment.
>
> (Shanmugaratnam, 2014)

Central to the lifting of productivity is the role to be played by SMEs. In Singapore, these SMEs employ 70% of all workers, account for 50% of economic output, and 99% of all businesses. The 2015 Singapore Budget announced that the government will spend S$5.5 billion over the next five years in its efforts to improve productivity efforts. Most of these funds are provided through generous subsidies, grants, and financial incentives to SMEs to reduce their reliance on foreign labour and improve productivity practices. These schemes are summarised in Box 2.1.

There is limited empirical data that is publicly available to evaluate the efficacy of these programmes in raising productivity. In addition to these measures, the government introduced reforms to expand tertiary education participation rates as well as programme of skills upgrading.

In 2011 the government announced that it would make available 2000 additional university places between 2011 and 2015 at Singapore's four universities: National University of Singapore (NUS), Nanyang Technological University (NTU), Singapore Management University (SMU), and Singapore University of Technology and Design (SUTD). This would increase higher education participation from 26 to 30% by 2015. It also announced a Committee on University Education Pathways Beyond 2015, to explore avenues for increasing higher education participation beyond 30%. The Committee of University Education Pathways (CUEP) recommendations were accepted in 2012, and the government announced that two educational institutes, the Singapore Institute of Technology (SIT), a public institution which partners with foreign universities to deliver their courses in Singapore; and UniSIM, a private institution, would be given university status. They would now admit full-time students and be tasked with awarding their own degrees. This would enable the government to increase university seats by 3000 students a year by 2020 (Waring, 2014), and target a higher education participation rate of 40% by 2020.

In recognising the need for enhanced training, the government launched Skills Future in 2014, a skill upgrading programme, *Skills Future*. The programme is budgeted to spend S$ 1 billion annually until 2020 on improving skills of the domestic workforce through a range of training, development and certification programmes. Singapore citizens, of all age groups, can apply for a range of programmes and receive partial funding. In most cases the funding covers up to 90% of cost of the training programmes (subject to a ceiling). Singapore's Deputy Prime Minister, Mr Tharman Shanmugaratnam said:

> ...we will create a new environment for lifelong learning. It is critical to our future. It will develop the skills and mastery needed to take our economy to the next level. More fundamentally, it aims to empower each Singaporean to chart their own journey in life, and gain fulfilment at work and even in their senior years. We have called this development effort "Skills Future". It marks a major new phase of investment in our people, throughout life.
>
> (Skills Future, 2015: Part C)

The aim of the programme is to improve competitiveness by increasing skills and productivity of the workforce; to develop a strong Singapore-core workforce; to incentivise businesses to 'go lean'; get more done with less by relying on automation, mechanisation and relying on technological solutions

Further to the macro policy interventions to drive productivity at the industry level, trade associations incentivise firms as well. Associations such as the Singapore Business Federation (SBF) that are represented on the National Productivity and Continuing Education Council, chaired by the Deputy Prime Minister, work in tandem to develop strategies to achieve a 2–3% annual growth in productivity (Ipx1.com, 2018). To combat the very low productivity growth and rising business costs, SBF, in 2016, released a whole industry position paper for the creation of a vibrant Singapore with a pointed recommendation focused on reviewing Singapore's foreign labour policies. Further, it also called for a review and revision of the approach taken to developing and upskilling firms, adopting an entrepreneurial mind-set and grooming talent with the appropriate skillset and behaviours through programmes such as Skills Future.

In collaboration with the Singapore National Employers Federation (SNEF), SBF organises initiatives such as the National Productivity Month to disseminate information and industry best practices highlighting approaches to improve productivity at the firm level. Programmes such as Mentorship for Accelerating Productivity Program (MAP) are also in place to support firms with strategies relating to better human resource planning, customer service provision and developing in-house productivity champions. To reward firms that participate and are able to demonstrate improved productivity measures, SBF hosts the coveted Singapore Productivity Awards annually (SBF.com, 2018). In the manufacturing sector, the Singapore Manufacturing Federation (SMF) set up the Singapore Innovation and Productivity Institute (SIPI) as a one-stop shop 'knowledge enterprise to champion manufacturing excellence' through the provision of 'productivity resources, customised road mapping and coaching support' (SIPI.org, 2018).

2.4 Conclusion

The policy experience of Singapore potentially holds at least two important lessons for other countries with large populations of migrant workers. The first lesson is that the longer and the more significant the dependency on foreign labour, the more likely it is that a path dependency develops which is difficult to overcome through policy initiatives alone. Second, it is highly likely that a low wage/low skill, low productivity 'trap' emerges in vocational employment, where employers cannot attract young people (as wages are low and the work is considered menial) which, in turn, leads to continued dependence on low-cost foreign labour and significant disincentive to invest in skills or automation. These implications suggest that a new approach is needed in such countries if they are to modernise their economies and avoid the vexed challenges that faced the authorities in Singapore.

Notes

1 The age-specific resident male (female) labour force participation for those aged 55 to 59 is 88.7 (63.1) and for those aged between 60 and 64 is 76.9 (48.8) (Department of Statistics, 2017).
2 The GINI coefficient measures the statistical dispersion of wealth (or income inequality) in a country. It ranges from 0 to 1, with one indicating the highest inequality.
3 This in part is due to the tax treatment of mandatory contributions to an individual's provident fund. In 2018, these ranged between 37.5% of wages (for those below 55) to 12.5% (for those above 65) subject to a ceiling (Central Provident Fund Board, 2018).
4 Non-tax or, more generally, unconventionally-sourced income, has fluctuated between the very sizable shares of 25% and 35% over the past 15 years. Thus, policymakers have been successful in reducing the reliance on taxes in favour of unconventional sources of revenue. Unconventional sources of revenue are defined as 'sources such as regulatory levies and usage fees of public infrastructure and amenities, income from institutions such as sovereign wealth funds and profits from government-linked companies, and duties on activities such as lotteries' (Asher et al., 2015). See Kwan et al. (2016) for an assessment of Singapore's revenue and expenditure composition; and Asher (2005) and Asher and Bali (2017) on the role of unconventional sources of revenue in public financial management.
5 The Finance Minister, Tharman Shanmugaratnam, in his Annual Budget Statement noted: 'The basic reality is that these sectors which are most dependent on foreign workers are also the ones furthest behind international standards of productivity, and which account for the lag in productivity in our overall economy.'
6 www.todayonline.com/business/foreign-worker-levy-hikes-deferred-marine-process-sectors
7 Singapore Parliament, 'Foreign Workers (Particulars)', 14 March 1984.
8 All citizens and permanent residents are required to participate in the Central Provident Fund. Individuals and their employers contribute up to 12.5–37.5% of their monthly wage (subject to a wage ceiling that varies across the age of a member). Largely during periods of economic instability, the Singapore Government has made parametric changes to the contribution rate that employers have to pay. This temporarily reduces labour costs, while leaving the 'take-home' pay of the employee unaffected. See Asher and Bali (2013) for a detailed review.

References

Ang, S., Van Dyne, L. and Begley, T. (2003) The employment relationships of foreign workers versus local employees: a field of study of organizational justice, job satisfaction, performance and OCB. *Journal of Organizational Behaviour*, 24(5), 561–583.

Asher, M.G. and Bali, A.S. (2013) Pension reforms in Singapore: assessing fairness and sustainability, *Malaysian Journal of Economic Studies*, 50(2), 175–191.

Asher, M.G. (2005) Mobilizing non-conventional budgetary resources in Asia in the 21st century. *Journal of Asian Economics*, 16(6), 947–955.

Asher, M.G., Bali, A.S. and Kwan, C.Y. (2015) Public financial management in Singapore: key characteristics and prospects. *The Singapore Economic Review*, 60(03), 1550032.

Asher, M.G. and Bali, A.S. (2017) Creating fiscal space to pay for pension expenditure in Asia. *Economic and Political Studies*, 5(4), 501–514.

Athukorala, P. and Manning, C. (1999) *Structural Change and International Migration in East Asia: adjusting to labour scarcity*. Melbourne: Oxford University Press.

Au Yong, Hawyee (2014a) Singapore's Productivity Challenge: Part 1. Available at: https://lkyspp.nus.edu.sg/docs/default-source/case-studies/productivity-challenges-in-singapore-part-1.pdf?sfvrsn=ecca960b_2

Au Yong, Hawyee (2014b) Singapore's Productivity Challenge: Part 2. Available at: https://lkyspp.nus.edu.sg/docs/default-source/case-studies/productivity-challenges-in-singapore-part-2.pdf?sfvrsn=26ca960b_2

Au Yong, Hawyee (2014c) Singapore's Productivity Challenge: Part 3. Available at: https://lkyspp.nus.edu.sg/docs/default-source/case-studies/productivity-challenges-in-singapore-part-3.pdf?sfvrsn=8aca960b_2

Au Yong, Hawyee (2014d) Singapore's Productivity Challenge: Part 4. Available at: https://lkyspp.nus.edu.sg/docs/default-source/case-studies/productivity-challenges-in-singapore-part-4.pdf?sfvrsn=eec9960b_2

Barro, R.J. (1996) *Determinants of Economic Growth: a cross-country empirical study* (No. w5698). National Bureau of Economic Research.

Central Provident Fund Board (2017) Annual Report. Available at: www.cpf.gov.sg/Members/AboutUs/about-us-info/annual-report (accessed 14 August 2018).

Chen, E.K. (1997) The total factor productivity debate: determinants of economic growth in East Asia. *Asian-Pacific Economic Literature*, 11(1), 18–38.

Department of Statistics, Government of Singapore (2017) *Singapore Yearbook of Statistics*. Available at: www.singstat.gov.sg/publications/reference/yearbook-of-statistics-singapore

Economic Strategies Committee (2010) Report of the Economic Strategies Committee. Available at: www.mof.gov.sg/Portals/0/MOF%20For/Businesses/ESC%20Recommendations/ESC%20Full%20Report.pdf (accessed on 11 September 2018).

Hui, W.T. and Toh, R. (2014) Growth with equity in Singapore: challenges and prospects. Conditions of Work and Employment Series #48. Available at: www.ilo.org/public/libdoc/ilo/2014/114B09_32_fren.pdf Geneva: International Labour Organization.

International Monetary Fund (2018) *World Economic Outlook*. Washington DC: International Monetary Fund.

Ipx1.com. (2018) About NPCEC. Available at: http://ipx1.com/WayToGo_SF6/about-npcec (accessed 14 August 2018).

Krugman, P. (1994) The myth of Asia's miracle. *Foreign Affairs*, 62–78.

Kwan, C.Y., Bali, A.S. and Asher, M.G. (2016) Organization and reporting of public financial accounts: insights and policy implications from the Singapore budget. *Australian Journal of Public Administration*, 75(4), 409–423.

Lim, L.Y. (2016) Fifty years of development in the Singapore economy: an introductory review. In *Singapore's Economic Development: Retrospection and Reflections*, pp. 1–15

Low, D. and Vadaketh, S.T. (2014) *Hard Choices: challenging the Singapore consensus*. Singapore: National University of Singapore Press.

Ministry of Manpower (2008) Foreign Workers Relocated to Approved Accommodation upon MOM's Intervention. Press Release. Available at: www.mom.gov.sg/newsroom/press-releases/2008/1370-foreign-workers-relocated-to-approved-accommodation-upon-moms-intervention (accessed 11 September 2018).

Ministry of Manpower (2011) Two Dormitory Operators Fined for Aiding Employers to House Foreign Workers in Unacceptable Accommodation. Press Release Available at: www.mom.gov.sg/newsroom/press-releases/2011/two-dormitory-operators-fined-for-aiding-employers-to-house-foreign-workers-in-unacceptable-accommodation (accessed 16 January 2016).

Ministry of Manpower (2012) Two Managers Slapped with Hefty Fine for False Declaration in Foreign Worker Housing Database. Available at: www.mom.gov.sg/newsroom/press-releases/2012/two-managers-slapped-with-hefty-fine-for-false-declaration-in-foreign-worker-housing-database (accessed 16 January 2016).

Ministry of Manpower (2015) Labour Force in Singapore 2014. Available at: www.mom.gov.sg (accessed 23 May 2015).

Ministry of Manpower (2016) Two Construction Companies Fined $180,000 in Total for False Declaration and Foreign Worker Housing Offences. Press Release. Available at: www.mom.gov.sg/newsroom/press-releases/2016/0304-two-construction-companies-fined-for-false-declaration (accessed 16 January 2016).

Ministry of Manpower (2018) *Yearbook of Manpower Statistics 2018*. Available at: http://stats.mom.gov.sg/Pages/Singapore-Yearbook-Of-Manpower-Statistics-2018.aspx

Ministry of Trade and Industry (2017) Economic Survey of Singapore. Available at: www.mti.gov.sg/ResearchRoom/Pages/Economic-Survey-of-Singapore-2017.aspx

OECD (2011) Part-time Employment. OECD Statistics. Available at: www.oecd.org (accessed 28 March 2012).

Pang, E.F. and Lim, L.Y. (1982) Foreign labour and economic development in Singapore. *International Migration Review*, 16(3): 548–576.

Pang, E.F. and Lim, L.Y.C. (2015) Labor, productivity and Singapore's development model. *The Singapore Economic Review*, 60(03), 15500331-30.

Pang, E.F. and Lim, L.Y.C. (2016) Labour, Productivity and Singapore's Development Model. Chapter 7, pp. 135–168. In Linda Lim (ed.) *Singapore's Economic Development.* Singapore: World Scientific.

SBF.com. (2018) Position Paper for a Vibrant Singapore – Summary Sheet. Available at: www.sbf.org.sg/images/pdf/2016/Position_Paper_Summary_Sheet.pdf (accessed 14 August 2018).

SBF.com. (2018) Productivity. Available at: www.sbf.org.sg/capability-building/productivity (accessed 14 August 2018).

Shanmugaratnam, T. (2013) A Better Singapore: Quality Growth, An Inclusive Society, FY2013 Budget Statement. Available at: www.singaporebudget.gov.sg/budget_2013/pc.html (accessed 9 June 2015).

Shanmugaratnam, T. (2014) Opportunities for the Future', FY 2014 Budget Statement. Available at: www.singaporebudget.gov.sg/budget_2014/home.aspx (accessed 9 June 2015).

SIPI.org. (2018) About Us. Available at: www.sipi.org.sg/index.php/about-us/ (accessed 14 August 2018).

Skills Future (2015) Budget Speech 2105 – Section C: Developing Our People. Available at: www.skillsfuture.sg/speeches.html/lbudget-speeche-2015.html (accessed 17 September 2016).

Tan, K.S. and Bhaskaran, M. (2016) The Role of the State in Singapore: pragmatism in pursuit of growth. Chapter 4, pp. 51–82, in Linda Lim (ed.) *Singapore's Economic Development.* Singapore: World Scientific.

Today (2017) Foreign worker levy hikes deferred for marine, process sectors. 21 February 2017. Available at: www.todayonline.com/business/foreign-worker-levy-hikes-deferred-marine-process-sectors

Tsao, Y. (1985) Growth without productivity: Singapore manufacturing in the 1970s. *Journal of Development Economics,* 19(1–2), 25–38.

Vadaketh, S.T. and Low, D. (2014) *Hard choices: Challenging the Singapore consensus.* NUS Press.

Vu, M.K. (2013) The Dynamics of Economic Growth: policy insights from comparative analyses in Asia. Cheltenham: Edward Elgar.

Vu, M.K. (2014) Singapore's Economic Growth Patterns and Productivity Performance Paper Presented at the 10th Anniversary of the LKY School of Public Policy, 17 October 2014.

Waring, P. (2014) Singapore's global schoolhouse strategy: retreat or recalibration? *Studies in Higher Education,* 39(5), 874–884.

World Bank (2018) World Development Indicators. Available at: www.worldbank.org

Yap, M.T. and Gee, C. (2016) Singapore's Demographic transition, the labour force and government policies: the last fifty years. Chapter 9. pp. 195–219, in Linda Lim (ed.) *Singapore's Economic Development.* Singapore: World Scientific.

Yeoh, B. (2007) Singapore: Hungry for Foreign Workers at All Skill Levels. Working Paper, National University of Singapore, Singapore.

3 Research method

3.1 Chapter aim and research questions

The objective of the research project was:

> To characterise industry performance in areas of innovation and productivity through the establishment of the top 5 to 8 indicators in operational performance and building a good benchmarking database of 200 local SME manufacturing and engineering companies.

This chapter justifies and describes the research approach taken to address this objective and defines the associated research questions. These questions were developed in the national context of concern for the relatively poor productivity performance of Singaporean SMEs with regard to other nations in Asia. The basis for the questions lies in the neoclassical economic theory behind a nation's production function. Here, productivity growth depends mainly on the accumulation of capital and labour. But, when these inputs are held constant, economists (e.g., Solow, 1956) have explained that growth can still occur through 'residual' inputs like technology. Measures of these residuals are termed the growth of total factor productivity; they vary from country to country and between time periods but are mostly positive. Hence, when these measures remain constant or begin to fall, nations like Singapore become seriously concerned about the impact on social and economic development. Consequently, the project's research questions orientate around assisting policy makers to understand the underlying elements of productivity performance. These were:

1. What are the key drivers of Total Factor Productivity (TFP) amongst SMEs in the Singaporean manufacturing sector?
2. How can these drivers be used to understand the state of competitiveness of Singaporean SMEs in the manufacturing sector?

3. How can these drivers be used to develop a mechanism for observing the evolution of SMEs' productivity and innovation?

These 'nested' questions are of the 'what and how' type, and their exploratory and descriptive nature suggested a particular research approach (Dubois and Gadde, 2001), given the philosophical understanding that impacted the research (Schwandt, 2000). From competing epistemological paradigms, an interpretative phenomenological approach was adopted, as an understanding was sought of 'social action in order to arrive at a causal explanation of its course and effects' (Weber, 1947). This was considered optimal for studying the social world and the relationships of SMEs within it, especially given the limited time duration defined by the sponsor for the project. Neatly coupled to this approach, social constructivism led the ontological enquiry, because 'reality' came from the construction of knowledge through the everyday experiences of humans (Charmaz, 2000) e.g., what SME leaders felt about initiatives to foster innovation. Such accumulation of knowledge, and our understanding of it, is denoted in question 1 – the 'what'. The enactment of that knowledge is denoted in questions 2 and 3. These two philosophical positions are commonly adopted in tandem in empirical research and point to an inductive approach, involving a qualitative data collection process (e.g., the collection of opinions) in preference to a quantitative one (e.g., the collection and analysis of aggregate statistics).

3.2 Research framework

The overall research framework deployed to articulate with the above philosophical stance is depicted in Table 3.1.

This framework is modelled on the Gioia method. This has proved rigorous and robust across many projects. However, it has attracted some criticism. First, the extent of the transferability of its idiosyncratic findings to other domains has been questioned. In reply, Gioia, Corley and Hamilton (2013) have argued that all interpretative approaches, especially those studying the socially constructed structures and processes fashioned by its observed subjects (e.g., SME leaders) in a particular context (e.g., Singapore), contain unique findings, though transferability can occur when the context and subjects are similar (e.g., groups in similar cultural settings). Second, researchers might see the framework as an inflexible 'cookbook', that implies a strict implementation of stages and rules. This could lead to its inappropriate application to a certain phenomenon, in the way that a hammer always searches for a nail. Again, Gioia et al. (2013) refute this assertion and urge researchers to treat their framework for qualitative, inductive research as possessing inherent flexibility and an openness

Table 3.1 Profile of the research framework

Steps	Features
Research design	Articulation of well-defined phenomenon and research questions
	Engagement with literature, with suspension of judgement about its conclusions to allow discovery
	Triangulation of data collection to ensure the capture of multiple perspectives of the phenomenon
Data collection 1	Good voice extended to subjects as knowledgeable agents
	Preservation of flexibility of interview protocols based on subject's responses
	Allowing prior 'expert' subject knowledge to inform data collected from consequent subjects
Data analysis	Performance of initial data coding, maintaining the integrity of 1st-order subject terminology
	Development of a comprehensive compendium of 1st-order terms
	Organisation of 1st-order terms into 2nd-order themes
	Distillation of 2nd-order themes into overarching theoretical dimensions
	Assemblage of terms and themes into a set of survey questions
Data collection 2	Stratified random sampling to ensure population representativeness
	Enactment of survey questions, preserving flexibility of interview protocols based on responses
	'Live' recording and transcription to preserve accuracy of subject perception
	Cross-checking of subject recall through transcription inspection and correction
Data analysis 2	Investigation of extent of accuracy of initial themes by confirmatory analysis
	Content analysis of agreed responses
Ethical standing	Prior confirmation of research framework using detailed ethical framework
	Approval of ethical framework by Murdoch University (Australia) Research Ethics Committee

Source: Adapted from Gioia and Pitre, 1990, by the authors

to innovation, so it can be adjusted and developed to suit existing and new phenomena. Research in this project was based on such a flexible approach to the framework and, as its objective was to examine the state of the key drivers of competitiveness and to observe the perceptions and behaviour of SME leaders to them in a specific geographic context, the first critique is necessarily negated.

3.3 Data collection: Phase 1

The project adopted a two-phased data collection process. The first phase was designed to elicit and build contextual knowledge around the drivers of Total Factor Productivity and to identify the key ones, as they impacted on the competitiveness of Singaporean SMEs. To ensure that the study avoided bias from particular viewpoints, it employed multiple perspectives in a triangulated approach – one that is regarded highly in social science research. After collection, data from these different sources was coded, compared with each other and analysed for themes, following a systematic process guided by the following advice:

> From the beginning of data collection, the qualitative analyst is beginning to decide what things mean, noting regularities, patterns, explanations, possible configurations, causal flows and propositions. The competent researcher holds these conclusions lightly maintaining openness and skepticism, but the conclusions are still there, inchoate and vague at first then increasingly explicit and grounded.
>
> (Miles and Huberman, 1984, p. 11)

The triangulated approach adopted in phase 1 is summarised in Figure 3.1. Its output is a set of drivers of TFP and, after testing and refinement, these became the basis of the main survey in phase 2.

3.3.1 Extant literature

First, a critical literature review was conducted to identify both internal (i.e. firm specific) and external (e.g., national policies) causal factors driving the Solow residual for Singapore. Academic databases (i.e., Web of Science, SCOPUS, Google Scholar) were searched systematically. This search produced about 275 references.

3.3.2 SME interviews

Second, a sample of 20 SME leaders, selected at random by the project sponsor (the Singapore Innovation and Productivity Institute), was surveyed in order to examine their perspectives of extant policy and their particular entrepreneurial challenges. These interviews lasted between 1 and 2 hours and elicited detailed information on the business context in Singapore, their current productivity and innovation issues and ways of increasing their efficiencies. In summary, the leaders identified six areas of direct relevance:

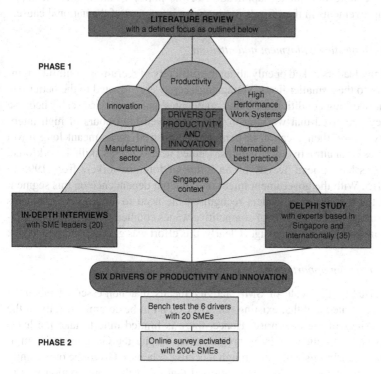

Figure 3.1 The triangulation of data collection
Source: Author's construction

a) Labour market reforms

Government policy to reduce the dependence of the city-state on foreign workers had two effects. First, individual SMEs reacted by bidding for home grown labour against other SMEs and larger organisations, so decreasing their bottom line through additional search costs and increased unit labour costs. Second, policy prescriptions made it difficult to employ foreign workers by raising the price of employment visas, thus impacting existing future base line costs directly. SME leaders were convinced that these aggregate labour cost increases did not translate into concomitant increases in productivity. Further, they asserted forcefully that the necessary labour force changes meant that business processes, including training and mentoring, were going to be tough to embed in the tight period defined by government. Notably, they agreed that while such changes were necessary to make Singapore more competitive over the long run, they called for a more incremental application of the policy to allow them to make improvements in their firm's productivity in support of the national cause.

b) Domestic employment and attrition

Many leaders talked openly about the difficulty of recruiting youthful engineers to their smaller firms. Young engineers were attracted to the better pay and working conditions of larger companies and the service sector because they perceived that working in SMEs involved long hours of high intensity. More, their location in peripheral industrial zones meant long travel times to unattractive destinations. Denied access to this skilled workforce, SMEs had to lean heavily on an influx of foreign workers from 1995 to 2015. With the government intent on reducing dependence on this segment of the labour force, leaders recognised the need to attract new graduates through an enticing mix of competitive wages coupled with a generous non-monetary incentive package. Clearly, this effort was going to increase costs.

c) Training opportunities

Inevitably, the scale of SME activity means that non-essential labour is not tolerated and that existing employees tend to be committed fully to the workings of the enterprise. Hence, there is limited time to take the leave necessary to attend training programmes, despite the Government's ambition to upskill its workers through incentive schemes. Given the opportunity costs of attendance, leaders confirmed that often their only option was to keep staff productive on the shop floor. However, leaders did appreciate the role of training in ensuring that their workers were cognisant of cutting edge production methods and that mind-sets were focused on continuous learning.

d) Automated production

The limitations of scale and the structures of existing business models acted as major constraints against driving productivity gains through automation, in the eyes of many Singaporean SME leaders. Automation delivers major gains over large production runs and the small batch nature of production works against these cost advantages. Even in higher-capital-to-labour ratio sectors like pharmaceuticals, SME production runs were not long enough to generate least cost production.

e) Government schemes

Many SME leaders had accessed government subsidies to upgrade their technological base, especially in buying advanced production machinery that would have been far too expensive to purchase by themselves. Although they admired the available schemes (e.g., Productivity and Innovation Credit) and incentives available, they found the application processes time-consuming and suffered from choice variety in finding the most appropriate scheme for them at their current phase of development.

f) Leadership succession

Singaporean leaders suffered from the SME's perennial problem – management succession. As leaders aged, they became concerned over the future of their businesses, in terms of strategic direction and governance. Simply, it seemed to them that there was no-one capable of taking the business forward. Moreover, deeply ingrained and tacit 'ways of doing business' meant that any new leader could not grasp the reins easily or quickly. In many cases, especially in family-run firms, the conservative and comfortable context and the focus on day-to-day survival meant that change was not at the forefront of strategic thinking.

3.3.3 Delphi study

A Delphi study was conducted to extract expert opinion from Government officials, policy makers and academics with insightful knowledge of SMEs. The Delphi technique was invented at the RAND Corporation in the USA during the Cold War. It is a convergence technique that involves several rounds of questions to a panel of experts in order to distil their knowledge with increasing homogeneity into an agreed answer. To avoid the inhibitions associated with face-to-face interviews, Delphi participation is anonymous and designed so that each expert has no knowledge of the identities of the other experts. In this project, 63 experts were approached with the round of survey questions of which 26 were Singapore-based experts. Instead of pursuing several rounds of questioning, there was so much convergence from the 28 usable responses that the Delphi was ended after round one. This round contained five trigger questions as follows:

Question 1	What are the most important drivers of TFP in SMEs?
Drivers *leadership* *human capital* *technology* *strategy* *government* *collaborative* *culture*	Respondents identified management quality and capabilities; learning mind-sets focused on skill development and utilisation within the labour force; pursuit of technical efficiency driven by product and process innovation; economic stability fostered by competitive exchange rates, market access and growth-oriented public policies; a conducive workplace culture, with high degree of employee participation and acceptance of change, that are known to drive productivity and innovation within an SME.

Question 2	In order of importance, what are the 5 most important drivers of innovation in SMEs?
Drivers *competitive forces* *leadership and culture* *skills and knowledge* *government* *collaboration*	Respondents identified competitive pressures to lower costs and survive in an industry; a culture of open communication and a spirit of innovation; solution-orientated work practices, increased organisational learning; protection of intellectual property, political stability, availability and access to global financial markets; and linkages with external bodies and centres of knowledge that are known to drive productivity and innovation within an SME.
Question 3	In order of importance, what are the 5 most important factors restricting innovation in SMEs?
Drivers *lack of innovation champions* *lack of innovation culture* *lack of enablers* *poor human capital* *lack of financial capital*	Respondents identified apathetic leadership, poor management styles, lack of strategic awareness; complacency, culture of fear, inability to manage failure and consistently reduced tolerance of risk-taking; insulation from competition, limited market access, and lack of policy support from the government to improve innovation; limited human and financial capital manifested in low skilled labour, limited education infrastructure, and limited resources to take financial risks were factors that restrict innovation within an SME.
Question 4	In order of importance, what are the 5 most important factors restricting productivity in SMEs?
Drivers *poor leadership* *lack of incentives* *technical inefficiency* *lack of competition* *lack of quality labour*	Respondents identified the lack of adequate vision and requisite soft skills in senior management; an undiluted focus on profits rather than creating value, limited appetite for risk and failure; outdated technology and primitive production lines; limited access to markets and inability to compete with dominant firms; systemic weaknesses in the labour force – including low levels of literacy and numeracy, motivation, and reduced incentives were factors that restrict productivity advancement within an SME.
Question 5	Would you kindly comment on other factors which you believe restrict productivity and innovation in SMEs?
Drivers *incentives and responses* *economies of scale* *innovation* *finance* *human capital*	Respondents identified the lack of incentives; issues related to poor market access and the inability to unleash gains from economies of scale; limited innovation processes and practices; lack of access to risk capital, limited integration with global markets and supply chains; and lack of willingness to fight unproductive labour, limited communication with the labour force were factors that inhibit productivity and innovation within an SME.

3.3.4 Results of Phase 1

As data from each of the three sources above was coded and added to discrete categories, the following key drivers of TFP in Singaporean SMEs emerged strongly:

- Technology and capital utilisation
- Pay and performance management
- Training, development and organisational learning
- Innovation culture
- Government policy, markets and regulation
- Leadership and management quality

The majority are internally and managerially controlled with external pressure provided mainly through government policy. To ensure their stability and authenticity, these drivers were bench-tested on a random sample of 20 different SMEs provided by the Singapore Manufacturers Federation (SMF). There was broad agreement amongst the leaders of these firms that the drivers were a good representation of productivity and innovation. The state of competitiveness of each driver is examined in phase 2.

3.4 Data collection: Phase 2

The second phase was designed to gather primary data from SME leaders on the outcome drivers of TFP from phase 1 (as depicted in Figure 3.1) using a survey of a large sample of SMEs. A stratified random sample was drawn from the Accounting and Corporate Regulatory Authority (ACRA) database – a directory of all businesses in Singapore with their respective Singapore Standards and Industry Classifications (SSIC) codes, allowing a finely grained selection from industry sub-sectors. To ensure sample representativeness, randomness, and the maximisation of response rate, speed and quality, the following process was adopted:

a) Purchase of the ACRA database – the most representative available
b) Contact of a random sample of 230 SMEs from this database, in proportion to the share of economic contribution of the industrial sub-sector to total manufacturing output in Singapore. The sub-sectors and firms sampled are displayed in Table 3.2.
c) Sample filtering to include SMEs that had been in business for 3 years and a prime manufacturer – this process led to a final sample of 215 firms
d) Sending of a project information binder to each firm in this 'cleaned' sample. The binder contained: (a) an information sheet about the project; (b) a hard copy of the survey; (c) an ethics information sheet; (d)

Table 3.2 Industrial subsector and SSIC classification codes

Industrial subsector	SSIC classification (two digit level)	Sample size 215
Chemicals and chemical products	C20	25
Pharmaceuticals and biological products	C21	7
Computer, electronic and optical products	C26	47
Fabricated metal products	C25	32
Food and beverage	C10; C11	8
Machinery and equipment	C28	71
Transport manufacturing/engineering	C30	17
Other (not classified)		8

Note: 80% of manufacturing capacity in Singapore is represented by these subsectors.

a news report about the project; and (e) a letter from the Singapore Manufacturing Federation, which encouraged all SMEs to participate in the project

e) Telephone calling that offered a $100 voucher as an incentive to participate

f) Semi-structured interviews conducted by two trained research associates (RAs), who were selected from the best final year students at the SMF Institute of Higher Learning. They used tablet computers (iPads) – to check for consistency, each interview was monitored by a cloud-based survey administrator, as the material was transmitted to headquarters in 'real time' during each interview. There were four teams of two RAs deployed who were paid an hourly rate and an incentive bonus for each appointment secured. On average, interviews took about 30 minutes

g) Cascade sampling by asking contacted SMEs in the sample to introduce the project to their network while holding the proportion of sector to total manufacturing constant

This data collection process, which totalled about 5 months, enjoyed considerable success with over 220 firms contributing responses; with the deletion of a few spurious observations, this resulted in a reliable sample of 215 firm level responses.

3.5 Conclusion

Based upon the Gioia framework, the adopted method contained sufficient flexibility to allow the sampling to evolve while, at the same time, preserving robustness in process through data triangulation, driver analysis and testing, driver refinement, sample representativeness and the incorporation of measures to boost response rates, speed, quality and consistency through the 'real time' supervision or researchers at the point of data collection. Given the enactment of a well-regarded social science framework underpinning the project and the successful results emerging from it, the project sponsor (SIPI) at the Singapore Manufacturers Federation affirmed their confidence in the method adopted, the professionalism of its implementation and the results obtained, and they duly signed off this stage of the project. The results of the stratified random sample of SME leader interviews in phase 2 formed the basis of the analysis of drivers of TFP, which is presented in Chapter 4.

References

Charmaz, K. (2000) Grounded theory: objectivist and contructivist methods. In: *The Handbook of Qualitative Research*. Edited by N.K. Denzin and Y. Lincoln. Thousand Oaks, CA: Sage Publications, Inc.

Dubois, A. and Gadde, L-E. (2001) Case studies in business market research. In: Woodside, A. (Ed). *Handbook of Business Market Research, Advances in Marketing and Purchasing*, Vol. 9, Cambridge: JAI Press.

Gioia, D. and Pitre, E. (1990) Multiparadigm perspectives on theory building. *Academy of Management Review*, 15(4), 584–602.

Gioia, D., Corley, K. and Hamilton, A. (2013) Seeking qualitative rigor in inductive research: notes on the Gioia methodology. *Organizational Research Methods*, 16(1), 15–31.

Miles, M.B. and Huberman, A.M. (1984) *Qualitative Data Analysis: a sourcebook of new methods*. California: Sage Publications Inc.

Solow, R.M. (1956) A contribution to the theory of economic growth. *The Quarterly Journal of Economics*, 70(1) (Feb 1956), 65–69.

Schwandt, T.A. (2000) Three epistemological stances for qualitative inquiry. In N.K. Denzin and Y.S. Lincoln (Eds.), *Handbook of Qualitative Research* (2nd ed., 189–213). Thousand Oaks, CA: Sage.

Weber, M. (1947) *Theory of Economic and Social Organisation*. Trans. A.M. Henderson and T. Parsons. New York: Oxford University Press.

4   Research findings

This chapter exhibits the findings from the project. An examination of the descriptive statistics around the sample of firms begins the process. This is followed by a detailed discussion of the six drivers of total factor productivity that emerged from phase one of the research project and were investigated during phase two. Finally, the method used to develop the: a) measures of firm competitiveness on each driver; and b) aggregated driver composite score, is described before the composite scores for each firm are revealed.

4.1 Descriptive statistics

The Singapore Government, through its Ministry of Trade and Industry agency 'SPRING', supports its small and medium enterprise to grow and helps to generate consumer confidence in their products and services. SPRING has informed SMEs to monitor ten key indicators regularly – these are defined in Table 4.1 below.

Varying components of total factor productivity are captured in these measures. In this study of 215 firms, most of the indicators were monitored across the specified sectors (Figure 4.1). The main tracking was done on profit margin (91%), with evidence that the local labour market tightening had spurred SMEs to monitor two of the three labour ratios (labour cost/employee and labour cost competitiveness) closely – at 76% and 70% respectively. This may have been done at the expense of the capital measures (capital intensity and capital productivity) which had less than 50% support, while value added to sales joined the less monitored ratios. Furthermore, the survey results contained a range of descriptive factors (e.g., employment, capital investment) reflecting their performance over the year prior to the survey implementation.

The majority of SMEs witnessed static employment levels in the preceding year, with around one-third claiming to have increases (Figure 4.2). Manufacturing operations, rather than customer service, enjoyed larger

Table 4.1 SPRING performance measures in Singaporean SMEs

Labour Cost Competitiveness measures the efficiency and effectiveness of the organisation in terms of its labour costs and is measured as a ratio of value added over total labour cost.

Labour Cost per Employee measures the average remuneration per employee and is measured by total labour costs divided by number of employees.

Labour Productivity measures the effectiveness and efficiency of employed labour, and is measured as a ratio of the value added (output) by the number of employees.

Sales per Employee measures the efficiency and effectiveness of marketing strategy, and is measured as a ratio of total sales by the number of employees.

Sales per Dollar of Capital measures the efficiency and effectiveness in fixed assets in the generation of sales and is measured by total sales divided by the value of fixed assets.

Value Added-to-Sales Ratio measures the proportion of sales created by the organisation over the cost of purchased material – i.e. the monetary value associated with the firms' production process. It is measured as a ratio of value-added over total sales.

Capital Intensity measures the extent to which the organisation or business is capital intensive and is measured as a ratio of the value of fixed assets to the number of employees.

Capital Productivity measures the efficiency and effectiveness of fixed assets in the generation of value added – i.e. the ratio of value added over the value of fixed assets.

Profit Margin measures the proportion of sales left to the organisation after deducting all cost and is measured as a ratio of operating profit over sales.

Profit-to-Value Added Ratio is a productivity measure that separates profit from the other components of value added (e.g., wages and salaries) and is measured as a ratio of the operating profit to the value added.

---

growth rates; while reliance on foreign contract workers was mostly stable or increasing. Many firms (over 51%) improved capital investment spending, though this was not concomitant with equivalent rises in either Research or in Development. As expected in small manufacturing firms, activity was marginally greater in the latter than the former.

Firms also witnessed greater increases in operational labour and non-labour costs than in either sales or total revenues (Figure 4.3). The Government's policy to control the amount of foreign labour caused a tighter national supply side market and this contributed directly to the wage bills of many firms. More importantly, competitiveness suffered a further set back as these labour cost hikes outpaced any gains in labour productivity. Clearly, if declines in this key element of the 'residual' were allowed to persist, national competitiveness of the Singaporean SME sector would be challenged greatly.

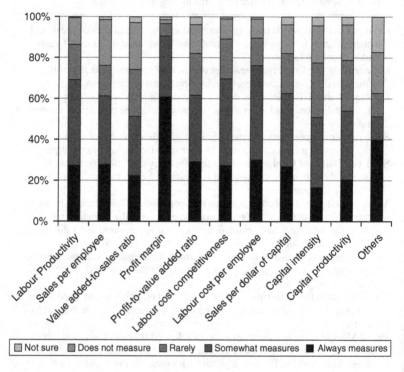

Figure 4.1 Measurement of operational indicators

Private, multiple owner firms dominated the sample (over 55%), but a significant minority were family-owned, partnerships or sole proprietorships (over 37%). The former firms are likely to have the bulk of their equity in family hands, where the first child inherits the shareholding – the practice of primogeniture (Figure 4.4).

4.2 SME driver performance

4.2.1 Technology and capital utilisation

Economists are in strong agreement on the main determinants of growth in modern economies (Jorgenson, Kuroda and Nishimizu, 1987; Mankiw, Romer and Weil, 1990; Vu, 2013). In particular, capital and its use in leading edge technologies like automated production systems, should increase both quality and consistency of product and production speed

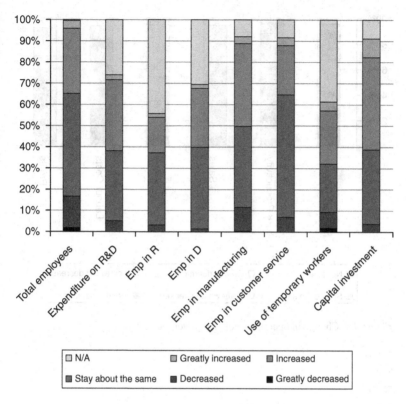

Figure 4.2 Change in operating indicators over the past year

(ceteris paribus) – both of which lead directly to higher productivity. The descriptive results discussed in Section 4.1 above provided a hint that the Singaporean SMEs might not be ahead of the pack when it comes to the deployment of high technology in manufacturing e.g., CNC (computer numerically controlled) machinery. The survey data confirm this pessimistic finding with only a small cohort (13%) claiming that their facilities were 'state of the art', with most (80%) claiming a satisficing condition around the industry average (Figure 4.5). Sadly, given the dominating contribution of the manufacturing sectors (machinery and metals; manufacturing engineering; metal products) to the national economy, this does not auger well for future competitiveness.

Despite little appetite for robotic manufacturing technology, customer relationship management software, CNC machinery, or enterprise resource

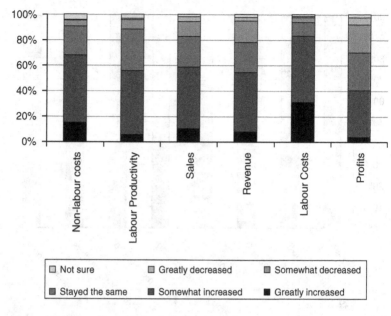

Figure 4.3 Change in operating indicators over the past year

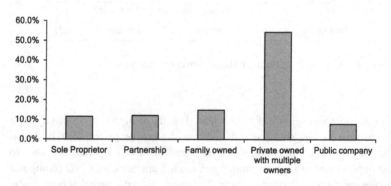

Figure 4.4 Ownership structure of the SMEs

systems on the production line, SMEs are keen users of smaller, peripheral technologies like hand-held computers and smart phones (87%), and cloud-based protocols (51%) (Figure 4.6). However, it is not likely that the appeal of these peripherals will translate into the significant corporate productivity gains necessary to drive the economy into a strong position relative to others in South East Asia. Without a significant upgrade in major production

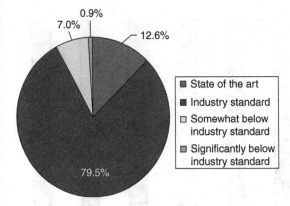

Figure 4.5 Level of technology in the firm's operations

technologies, these firms will not cope well with the increased labour costs consequent on the government's policy in reducing foreign workers. Shifts to capital intensive systems would reduce reliance on both domestic and foreign labour, whilst providing a much higher customer regard for the quality of Singapore's products and services.

This progress may not be achieved easily without government intervention. Sample firms claimed that such a central influence, coupled with their limited knowledge of new technologies and the ability of their senior managers to find advanced technical solutions, determined their ability to invest in cutting edge technology (Figure 4.7). Certainly, government can take on a more interventionist role e.g., by matching firms to technical solutions and by providing financial incentives. But, SME leaders are likely to invest more in such solutions, and more regularly, if they can see the directly derived benefits on productivity and quality for themselves. This suggests a more proactive role in competitive benchmarking, both inside and outside the nation state, perhaps through the use of external consultants – which many of them (44%) have never tried at all. Ironically, nearly 50% of them suggested that they assessed new technologies on a regular basis, but still failed to make investments in it. So, though awareness may be relatively high, other constraints may come into play. The search descriptors for new technology are highlighted in Table 4.2.

4.2.2 Pay and performance management

Many modern organisations utilise high-performance work systems (HPWS) that are designed to increase both productivity and innovation when these are linked directly to pay and performance. In these high-performance

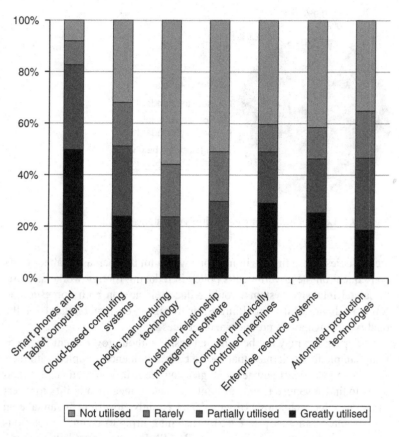

Figure 4.6 Technology practices within the firm

workplaces, employers attempt to forge a culture that inspires innovative activity. Employees are granted sufficient autonomy to suggest, and create, new ideas and ways of doing things. The effectiveness of such cultures depends heavily on the design and fair implementation of a combination of rewards, discretion and incentives for employees. This culture should reflect a deep organisational belief in continuous improvement in the use of capital and labour, a commitment to the generation of new knowledge, the application of 'state of the art' technology and the development of a proactive, learning mind-set.

The largest section of employees in this sample (see Figure 4.8) were production workers (66%) and most of these were engineers (20%) – these

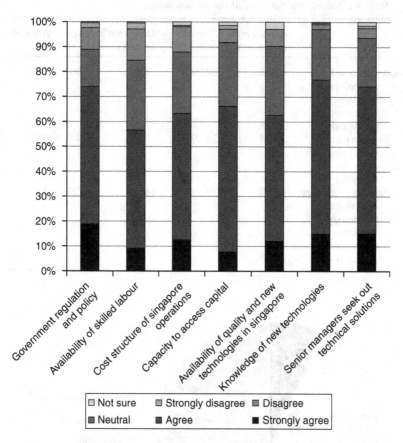

Figure 4.7 Determinants of investments in new technologies within firms

figures reflect the norm in the global population of SMEs. But, the dominance of production workers to engineers in this sample of 'manufacturing'
SMEs is noteworthy. This result might describe firms with low investments
in production technology and low skill sets amongst its workforce e.g., the
widespread use of cheaper foreign labour with no access to skill upgrading.
Reinforcing this view, many SME leaders claimed to be on the fringe of
what constitutes a true HPWS. However, there was plenty of evidence of
simple performance target setting and bonus systems in operations – in 50%
of firms, between 0 and 20% of production workers gained between 0 and
20% of their salary through bonuses and in 30% of firms, this figure rose to
21–40% of salary. Markedly, nearly 33% of SMEs had never or rarely used

Table 4.2 Search descriptors of SMEs for new technology

	At least once in 6 months	Annually	More than annually	Never	Not sure
Assess new technological solutions to improve productivity	46.0%	34.0%	8.8%	7.9%	3.3%
Benchmark with firms using 'state of the art' technology	30.2%	22.8%	9.3%	28.4%	9.3%
Appoint consultants to advise on technology solutions to improve productivity	14.0%	23.3%	14.0%	44.2%	4.7%

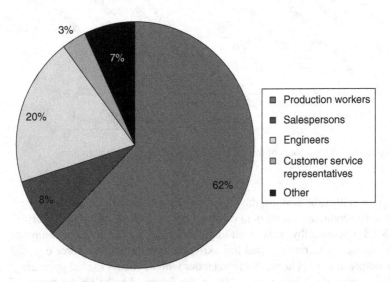

Figure 4.8 Breakdown of employment groups across SMEs

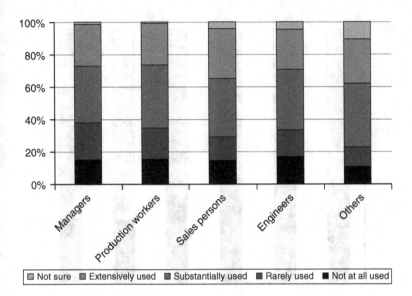

Figure 4.9 Use of formal performance appraisal systems

regular performance appraisal of employees (Figure 4.9). The degree of use did not waiver much between the types of employees in the firm's hierarchy – suggesting that its use is a variable that is culturally bound across a firm.

Such formal and regular employee feedback is recognised to be beneficial in the development of employees, helping to boost their individual productivity and aiding their problem-solving skills (Earley, Northcraft, Lee and Lituchy, 1990; Ghorpade, 2000 and Meyer, 1991). Though the engagement of Singaporean SMEs with true HPWS is limited, many leaders stated that they provided rewards for employee practices that helped increase productivity and innovation e.g., flexible task working; business process ideas generation and cross-team collaboration. Pointedly, few firms (<20%) stated that they rarely or never rewarded their staff for such contributions (Figure 4.10).

4.2.3 Training, development and organisational learning

An integral part of any HPWS is the constant upgrading of employee skills and competences through regular investments in training and development schemes (TDS). Such schemes can harness and reinforce learning to keep

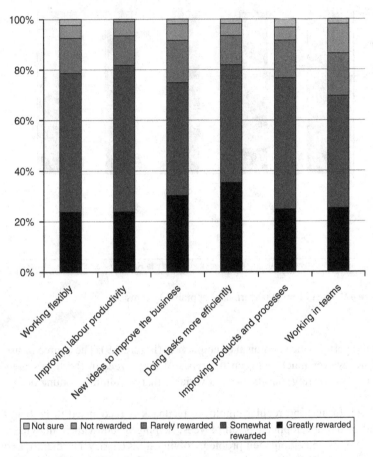

Figure 4.10 Use of incentives to improve productivity and innovation

mind-sets active and help to improve productivity and innovation through ideation. An increasing emphasis on health and safety and consumer demands for consistently high-product quality mean that TDS are imperative in manufacturing businesses. In particular, they help build and reinforce a learning culture that prevents firms from ossifying and lagging behind the competition. SME leaders reported high levels of employee activity and competence in work ethic, team working, IT familiarisation and skill accumulation. Given the more practical nature of work activity in manufacturing SMEs over that within service firms, it is no surprise that leaders shared

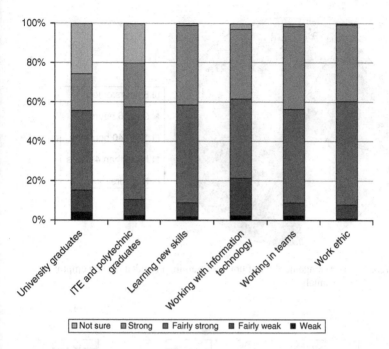

Figure 4.11 Quality and ability ratings across the workforce

a slight preference for the quality of graduates from vocational and poly-technic backgrounds over those from universities (Figure 4.11).

In 2013, Singapore's Ministry of Manpower claimed that each employee in its manufacturing sector got three days training per year. These results are less optimistic, with over 50% of leaders suggesting that provision in their SME was less than 2 days and a further 20% suggesting they provided between 2 and 5 days (Figure 4.12).

Increases in this domain represent a chance to lift productivity and innovation performance amongst SMEs, though the usual caveat in smaller firms applies: leaders may be keen on training, but they are often reluctant to remove employees from existing productive tasks on the shop floor. Indeed, the upskilling of senior management may suffer from a similar malaise, as over 80% of leaders claimed that they rarely, or do not, use formal programmes like MBAs (Figure 4.13). Many complained about problems experienced in the renewal of their own leadership through time, finding it difficult to attend shorter programmes like executive short programmes. Interestingly, few leaders used any form of performance management within

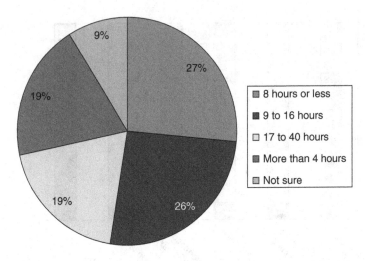

Figure 4.12 Average number of hours of training provided to each employee annually

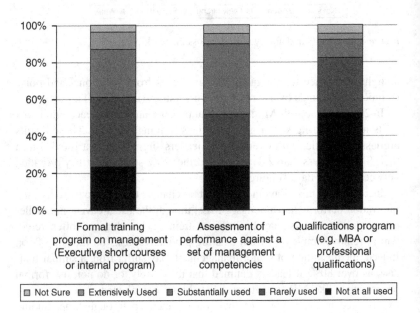

Figure 4.13 Use of management development mechanisms for senior management talent

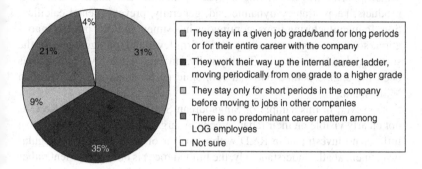

Figure 4.14 Career patterns within SMEs

their senior leadership teams – a strange feature, given their promotion of such systems amongst their junior managers and productive workforce. Such dysfunctionality could be due to firm size rather than motivation, with every executive working long hours to secure survival, rather than to chase rapid growth.

Clear career paths underpin a learning organisation. Movement across the functional areas of the firm creates a greater understanding of the demands of each for employees locked in one 'silo' over a career. Likewise, progression through the hierarchy provides a similar learning opportunity and requires new skills development, especially around decision-making and the management of individuals and teams. Clear pathways where employees moved vertically from grade to grade were only defined in around 30% of firms, though a further 30% suggested that employees did not progress at all, remaining in the same grade *ad infinitum* (Figure 4.14).

4.2.4 Innovation culture

The Oslo Manual describes innovation as:

> the implementation of a new or significantly improved product, or process ... marketing method, organizational method in business practices, workplace organization.
>
> (OECD 2005: p.46)

This comprehensive definition is adopted in this study, with its elements reflected in the survey instrument and in the notion of HPWS. As the root of many competitive advantages, active innovation practice allows organisations to improve business models, respond to competitive threats, seize opportunities in existing markets, penetrate new markets with new products, keep strategy dynamic and, generally, prevent mental calcification. In manufacturing firms, continuous investment in R&D propels innovation, so increasing productivity at the firm level and, on aggregate, at the sector and national levels. Traditionally, an innovative SME cohort has been the engine behind national economic performance e.g. the German Mittelstand.

However, in this sample of Singaporean SMEs, it is clear that R&D is not clearly visible on their radar screens. A large proportion (25–45%) have little or no investment in R&D with a quarter of firms making no regular investment at all. Understandably, the limited focus is on development rather than pure research. If firms cannot afford such investments, then collaboration with other agencies becomes an option. For instance, much leading-edge research occurs in research centres and often these are attached to universities, of which Nanyang Technological University in Singapore is a world leading exponent. However, the SMEs surveyed preferred to collaborate with other SMEs, rather than interact with universities. Moreover, the use of intermediary agencies, like consultants, can help match individual SMEs to new technologies, yet there was great reluctance amongst firms to use them. Even less expensive ways to invest, like crowdsourcing, were ignored. This satisficing approach may work well over the short run, but incrementally, these SMEs will fall behind 'state of the art' products, processes and business models. On a more promising note, these SMEs seemed to stay close to their customer and use that interchange to inform product or service development (Figure 4.15).

Previous findings suggested that SMEs in this sample engaged with HPWS irregularly and only at the periphery. There was little evidence to suggest that employees and middle managers were empowered to contribute ideas and engage in productivity improvements without hierarchical authority. It would seem that many SMEs may be ignoring the creative potential of their entire workforce when it comes to the generation, collation and enactment of new ideas. Many of these ideas come from the harnessing of failure in organisations. James Joyce (1922) said that 'A man of genius makes no mistakes. His errors are volitional and are the portals of discovery' and Sochiro Honda, founder of the Honda Motor Company, asserted that 'success can be achieved only through repeated failure and introspection.' In this sample, half of the leaders tolerated failure only 'sometimes'. This result, together with those that show risk taking and experimentation as relatively low, indicates a conservative culture amongst Singaporean SMEs (Figure 4.16).

Innovative feedback from employees has been gathered in meetings with senior management, who preferred an open-door policy on communications (Figure 4.17). But, it seemed that more formal gathering of feedback from

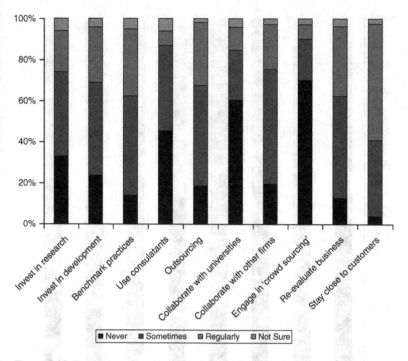

Figure 4.15 Frequency of innovative activities within the firms

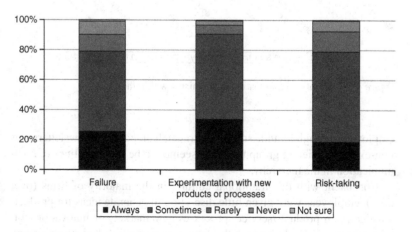

Figure 4.16 Levels of toleration in the firms

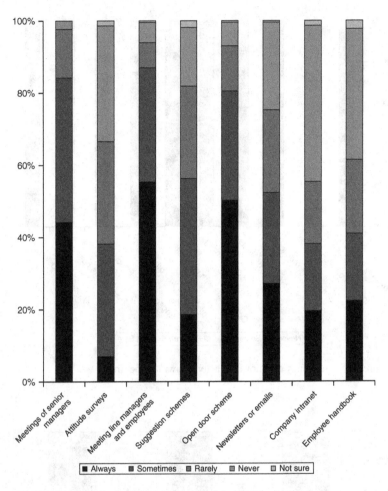

Figure 4.17 Use of communication mechanisms within the firms

employees through attitude surveys, intranet, handbooks or newsletters was non-existent. Briefing group meetings seemed to be the main lines of communication in the hierarchy.

Consistent with this traditional culture, in the majority of firms (over 60%), employees were given little discretion to generate ideas for productivity gains in products/service, processes/new markets or innovation policies (Figure 4.18). Indeed, in the latter, over one-fifth had no discretion at all.

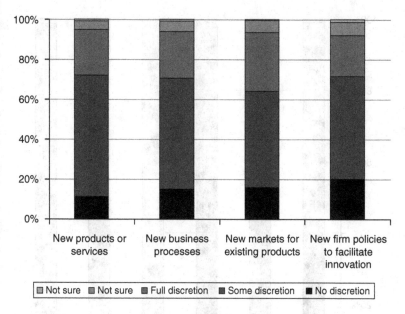

Figure 4.18 Employee discretion to develop innovation and productivity practices

4.2.4 Government policy, markets and regulation

For some economies, Singapore is a role model for integrated international-isation. Its geographic position provides a convenient hub for the oil and gas sector and for transportation. It has developed globally integrated financial markets and supply chains. Doing international business is made easier by minimal regulation and a range of reciprocal free trade agreements (FTAs). Despite this, SMEs have suffered as government reforms have privileged domestic labour to lower cost, foreign labour in a broader attempt to improve both manufacturing output and productivity.

To achieve its aims, a broad array of incentives has been provided. Sample evidence (Figure 4.19) indicates that SME leaders understand the Government's posture – over 90% had discussed firm productivity increases, and over 70% had discussed the building of an innovation culture. Further, the majority (85%) had availed themselves of financial schemes in the last year to address productivity, though a good proportion of them (50%) had not accessed the professional advice of productivity consultants or solution providers in this endeavour. There was a sense of do-it-yourself, as less than 10% had used productivity workshops or conferences to further their knowledge.

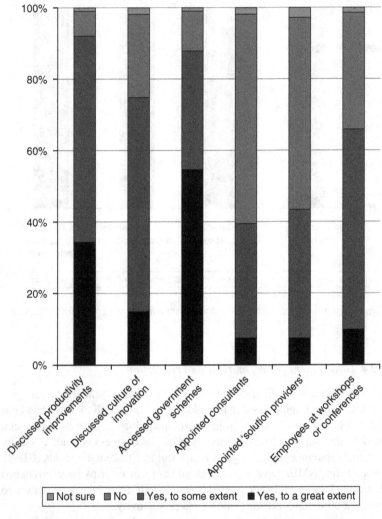

Figure 4.19 Firms' engagement with the Government's productivity agenda

The foreign labour component of firm productivity gave rise to a dilemma. On the one hand, the government was intent on reducing reliance on foreigners, but on the other, many SME leaders said that their business model would not survive such a policy, despite their attempts to follow it (Figure 4.20). About 70% of leaders reported a high or moderate reliance on foreigners, with leaders denying the assertion that such a reliance might create a 'dependence-effect' that would dampen their firm's propensity to innovate or become more productive.

Firms can reduce their reliance on foreign workers either through the substitution of capital for labour in the production process, for example through the use of robotics on the line, or through the costlier strategy of replacing foreigners with domestic workers. Either option (or even a mix of both) presents significant challenges of affordability and implementation – with its necessary downtime for the change-over from one system to another and the associated learning curve for snagging and operational adjustments. These production halts might be risky for many sample firms in terms of lost revenues and from customer impatience. Many leaders saw their smallness as problematic in this regard, though there was gratitude for the Government's helpful initiatives (e.g., Capability Development Grants and Productivity and Innovation Credit). Those firms taking advantage of the financial schemes saw benefits in productivity, investments in new technology, and the development of improved production techniques – all assisting in expanding the business (Figure 4.21).

Leaders (>80%) confirmed that the main driver of productivity and innovation was market competition, though over 50% claimed that the small size of the immediate market in Singapore restricted their ability to perform on both variables. To compensate, leaders thought that central government should reconsider its purchasing strategy to widen the market for them in the face of dominance by a few larger providers, and assist their entry into new markets, where the majority agreed that Singapore's FTAs were a bonus in facilitating new opportunities (Figure 4.22).

Many of the leadership and management issues in Singaporean SMEs stem from the reluctance of potential employees to work in the manufacturing sector, given the attractions of the financial, oil and gas and service sectors, locally. Consequently, as employers have relied on transient, foreign workers on short contracts, they have been reluctant to invest in formal, structured training and development programmes for them. Clearly, such investments in senior management training and upskilling can translate into better efficiency within the firm's operations which, in turn, advance productivity and performance. Moreover, better training in strategy can lead to more creative visions, clearer targets, stronger implementation and better monitoring and superior employee involvement and 'ownership'. As a result, the effectiveness of the firm in competitive markets should improve considerably.

Consistently across sectors, leaders claimed that they had a strong vision and strategy for their firms and set ambitious, stretched targets (Figure 4.23). As expected in any small manufacturing firm, leaders expressed a greater focus on attempts to improve productivity than on attempts to improve innovation. The great majority claimed that top performing employees were actively identified, developed and promoted and leaders did all they

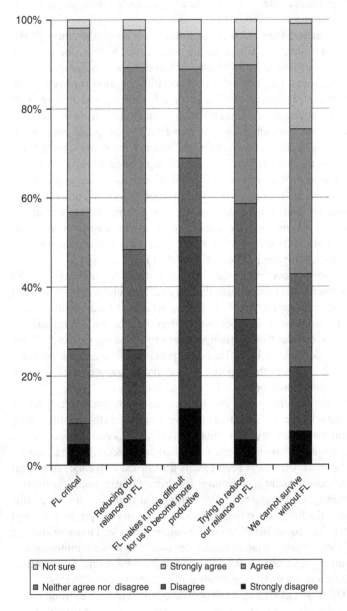

Figure 4.20 Reliance on foreign labour

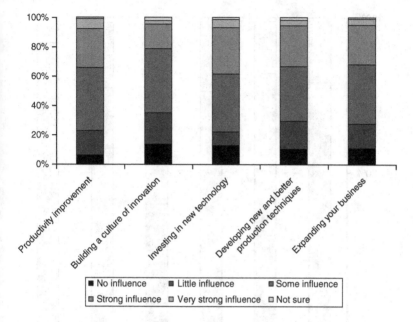

Figure 4.21 Impact of Government's financial schemes

could to retain such talent. Contrarily, leaders were less adamant that poorly performing employees were regularly identified and removed.

In terms of managerial skill sets (Figure 4.24), leaders claimed that their managers were skilled problem solvers. More, most managers were keen to listen to employees about their ideas in a culture that regularly promoted productivity improvements. Employees benefited from frequent conversations with their managers about individual performance, but leaders were dubious about management skill upgrading and their manager's ability to slow labour turnover. Again, these results suggest that work pressure in SMEs renders both leaders and managers time poor and so regular training and development is a luxury that is impossible to achieve.

4.3 Estimation of composite score

4.3.1 Method

A web portal was constructed to enable firms to interrogate their relative position within their sector and with other sectors, in terms of extant practices on innovation and productivity. To achieve a firm's original positioning, a three-step process was developed (see Figure 4.25).

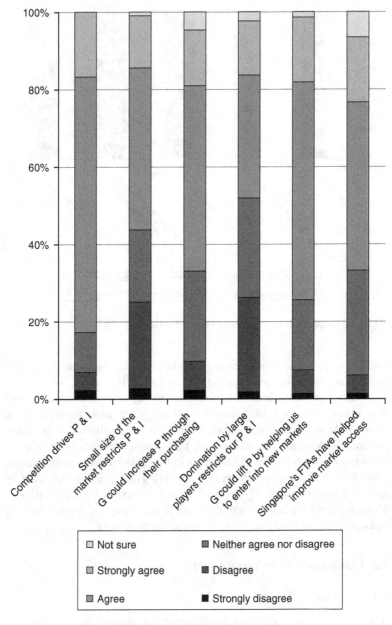

Figure 4.22 Public policy and productivity drivers in the Singapore economy

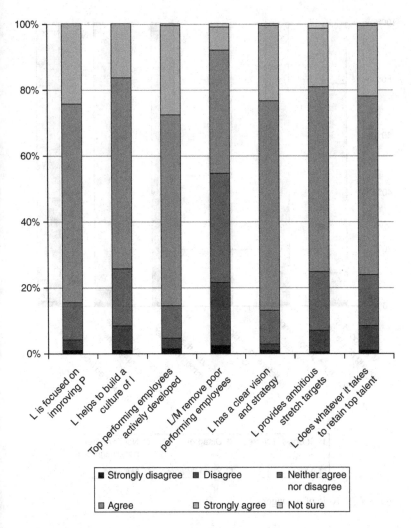

Figure 4.23 Role of leaders

a) Scoring questions

A maximum of seven questions (SQs) were identified from each of the six TFP drivers and these are scored by the leaders of firms. The responses that were most correlated to perceived best practice in advancing innovation and productivity were given a 100% score. Others were scored proportionately, given their perceived distance from this best practice.

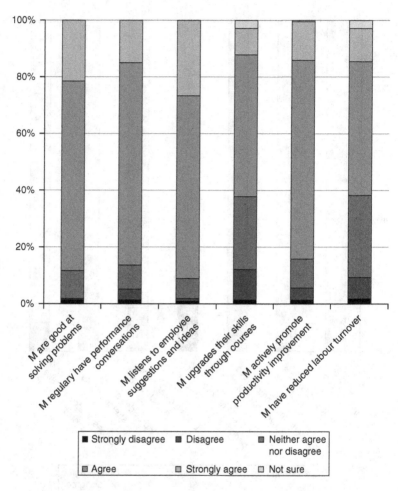

Figure 4.24 Role of managers

b) TFP driver score

The maximum of seven questions chosen for each TFP driver are scored and summed on the basis of a 1 to 10 Likert scale.[1] Each SQ was weighted equally in further calculations. For example, in the driver 'Training, development and organisational learning', five scoring questions were chosen. Each question was scored out of ten; the maximum score assigned to each SQ for this driver was ten divided by five, which equals two points.

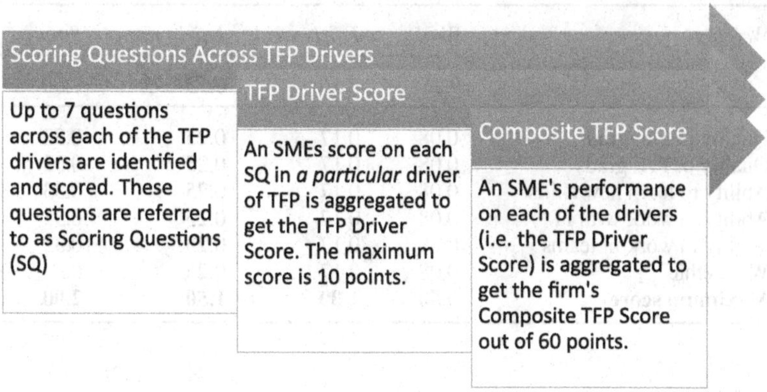

Figure 4.25 Three-stage method of calculating a composite score

For example, as shown in Table 4.3, leaders were asked to rank their employees across a number of variables on a scale consisting of: *Weak – Fairly Weak – Fairly Strong – Strong*, on the Training and Development driver. Each SQ on this driver equalled two points and this driver had six possible responses, hence each response equalled two divided by six or 0.33. This represents 100% of the score and equates to 'Strong' i.e. best practice in this sample. If leaders rated themselves as 'Strong' on each of the six possible responses, they accrued 100% of the score (0.33). On a Likert scale, the weighting reduces in proportion and so if leaders chose 'Fairly Weak' or 'Fairly Strong' for some answers, then these would be weighted 0.50 and 0.75 respectively. Response scores were then summed to find the SQ score. If a leader thought his firm was 'Strong' on everything, the summed score would be 2.0 (6 × 0.33) or if they thought they were weak across each element, they would score a sum of 0.50 (6 × 0.08).

The TFP driver scores by sector and driver are shown in Table 4.4, below. The scores range from an average of 3.7 in Food and Beverage for technological and capital utilisation to 7.4 in Pharmaceuticals and Food and Beverage for innovation culture. However, comparisons across these sectors should be made with caution, as each has different capital-output ratios and working practices and each sector faces specific regulations e.g., firms in the pharmaceuticals sector usually have high capital output ratios in the production of output than firms do in, say, the fabrication of metal products; pharmaceuticals is well known for its tight compliance regime. Though, even lower capital to labour employers contribute

Table 4.3 Example of scoring and summing for the TFP driver training and development

Weights	Weak	Fairly weak	Fairly strong	Strong
	0.25	0.50	0.75	1.00
Quality of Uni grads	0.08	0.17	0.25	0.33
Quality of ITE grads	0.08	0.17	0.25	0.33
Ability to learn new skills	0.08	0.17	0.25	0.33
Ability to work with IT	0.08	0.17	0.25	0.33
Ability to work in teams	0.08	0.17	0.25	0.33
Work ethic	0.08	0.17	0.25	0.33
Maximum score	**0.50**	**1.00**	**1.50**	**2.00**

significant output to the economy. Across the drivers, the ranges for individual scores are far tighter, from 0.8 (innovation culture and government policy and regulation) to 1.0 (training and development and leadership and management quality).

Building innovation cultures is the strongest performer according to leaders, followed by training and development and the quality of leadership and management development mid-ranking, with the utilisation and technology and capital and pay and performance in the lower rankings. Consisting mostly of firms that supply the marine industry, the Other Transport Equipment sector heads up the best practice for use of technology and capital; the F&B sub-sector leads on pay and performance management; Pharmaceuticals on training and development; F&B matching Pharmaceuticals on innovation culture; Computers and Electronics on engagement with the Government's productivity policy (as measured by access to schemes, attendance at workshops, etc.) and Pharmaceuticals on the quality of leadership and management. Some of the lower scores e.g., fabricated metal products on pay and performance and access to the Government's productivity agenda, might be explained by their greater reliance on lower cost foreign labour, rendering only a short run competitive advantage. Such sectors will likely be hit hard by the Government's current policy on privileging domestic labour.

c) Composite TFP driver score

Third, a composite score was generated, based upon the aggregation of these individual driver scores. This measure was called the *Composite TFP Score*. The theoretical range of scores on this measure stretched from 10 (equivalent to a score of 1 out of 10 on each driver) to 60 points (equivalent to a score of 10 out of 10 on each driver). The actual scores for SMEs across the sectors for Singapore ranged from 30.6 to 33.8 (Table 4.5). The highest average scores were recorded by Pharmaceuticals (33.8), Other Transport Equipment (32.6) and Computers and Electronics (32.5). Fabricated Metal Products (30.6) and the Machinery and Equipment (31.2) sub-sectors recorded the lowest scores. The average composite score was 31.9.

The usual caveats apply about assuming too much from these comparisons across sectors with different capital-output ratios.

4.3.2 Industry position

The cyclical fluctuations in macroeconomic data enter yearly productivity data because of the correlation between productivity growth and GDP growth. The fluctuations can be removed from time series data using statistical techniques like the Hodrick-Prescott Filter, so yielding true productivity influences on an economy's productivity growth trend. When used on Singapore's economy, annualised real productivity growth can be calculated. Figure 4.26 shows these de-cyclical calculations for both trend and annual rates of productivity growth for the overall economy and by sector in Singapore. They show two key things. First, for the overall economy, the trend productivity growth figures outweigh the annual ones, suggesting that recent productivity data was replete with cyclical influences. Second, the same hierarchy between trend and annual rates applied in the majority of sectors. Electronics had experienced low annual growth in productivity but once this was adjusted for fluctuation, it recorded a trend rate of 3.9%. Transport Engineering and Biomedical Manufacturing have experienced the highest annual and trends rates from 2010 to 2013 and these have achieved the highest composite score in the calculations for productivity and innovation practices in this survey.

4.3.3 Caveat

The sectors selected for this sample equate to around 90% of the value added by the Manufacturing establishment and about 60% of total establishments in Singapore. Together with the Composite Scores, these are detailed in Table 4.5. From 2010 to 2013, Electronics had low productivity growth per annum (Figure 4.22) but the highest share in value added and a fairly high Composite Score, while Food and Beverage suffered low productivity growth and had the lowest value added but a mid-ranked Composite Score. Hence, care must be taken in cross-comparisons from official statistics and the sample scores. For instance, the Composite Score calculated herein is not a measure of productivity nor a proxy for it. It is a leader's perception

Table 4.4 TFP driver scores by sector and driver

	Technology and capital utilisation	Pay and performance management	Training and development	Innovation culture	Government policy and regulation	Leadership and management quality
Computers and electronics	4.2	4.6	5.7	7	5.6	5.4
Pharmaceuticals	4.2	4.8	6.2	7.4	5.4	5.8
Chemicals and chemical products	3.9	4.6	5.6	6.9	5.2	5.6
Machinery and equipment	3.9	4.6	5.3	6.8	5.2	5.4
Food and beverages	3.7	5.2	5.9	7.4	5.3	4.8
Fabricated metal products	4.1	4.4	5.4	6.6	4.8	5.3
Other transport equipment	4.6	4.7	5.9	6.8	5.2	5.4
Others	3.8	4.3	5.2	7.2	5	5.2

Table 4.5 Select manufacturing statistics (2013) and composite scores

Sub-sectors	Share in total establishments	Share in value-added and rank	Key driver composite scores and rank
Food and beverages	9.0	4.0 (6)	32.3 (4)
Chemicals and chemical products	3.3	7.0 (4)	31.8 (5)
Pharmaceuticals and biological products	0.5	17.0 (2)	33.8 (1)
Fabricated metal products	14.2	5.0 (5)	30.6 (7)
Computer, electronic and optical products	3.4	34.0 (1)	32.5 (3)
Machinery and equipment	18.0	11.0 (3)	31.2 (6)
Other transport equipment	12.1	11.0 (3)	32.6 (2)
Total	60.5	89.0	

Source: Singapore Yearbook of Statistics (2014), and estimates from the authors

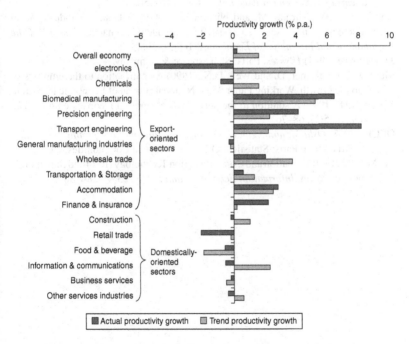

Figure 4.26 Annualised real productivity growth by sector, 2010–2013
Source: Adapted from the Economic Survey of Singapore Second Quarter, 2014

of how their firm follows best practice with regard to innovation and productivity. Further, though the official statistics presented in Figure 4.22 contain 'pro-cyclical' productivity data and techniques can be used to remove this and present a more natural picture of growth. The cross-sectional data captured in the Composite Scores is not amenable to such nuancing from statistical techniques and cannot provide similar estimations.

Note

1 A Likert scale is used in many social science studies to assess consumer preferences or opinions.

References

Earley, C.P., Northcraft, G.B., Lee, C. and Lituchy, T.R. (1990) Impact of process and outcome feedback on the relation of goal setting to task performance. *Academy of Management Journal*, 33(1), 87–105.

Ghorpade, Jai (2000) Managing five paradoxes of 360-degree feedback. *The Academy of Management Executive*, 14(1), 140–150.

Jorgenson, D.W., Kuroda, M. and Nishimizu, Z. (1987) Japan-US industry-level productivity comparisons, 1960–1979. of productivity change. *Journal of the Japanese and International Economies*, 1(1), 1–30.

James Joyce (1922) *Ulysses*. Paris: Shakespeare & Company.

Mankiw, N.G., Romer, D. and Weil, D.N. (1990) A contribution to the empirics of economic growth, Working Paper 3541, National Bureau of Economic Research.

Meyer, H.H. (1991) A solution to the performance appraisal feedback enigma. *The Executive*, 5(1), 68–76.

OECD (2005) *Oslo Manual: guidelines for collecting and interpreting innovation data*. 3rd edition. Paris: Statistical Office of European Communities, OECD.

Vu, M.K. (2013) Information and Communication Technology (ICT) and Singapore's economic growth. *Information Economics and Policy*, 25(4), 284–300.

5 Recommendations for policy and practice

The findings presented in this book help to contextualise and explain the aggregated productivity data for the manufacturing sector and the concerns expressed by the Singapore Government which are mirrored by other governments in the region. Productivity in Singapore has lagged behind international comparators in a number of sectors, including manufacturing. The findings presented in the previous chapter help us to understand the underlying reasons for this, and the main challenges faced by SMEs in the sector. Only by identifying deficits in the key drivers of Total Factor Productivity (TFP) can appropriate, and sometimes novel solutions be developed to renew productivity growth.

This chapter considers the practical initiatives that policy makers and industry can implement to help to enhance total factor productivity growth. Consistent with the approach throughout this text, the narrative is organised around each of the six key drivers with an exposition firstly of the policy recommendations and then, secondly, the practical advice offered to business leaders and managers on the micro-initiatives they may wish to deploy to enhance workplace level productivity. In both cases, recommendations flow from the productivity and innovation literature in addition to the key findings of our empirical study.

5.1 Improving technology and capital utilisation

Adopting technology solutions and upgrading capital in the production process is known to drive efficiency and improve productivity (see Vu, 2013; Faggio, Salvanes and Van Reenen, 2010). In particular, SMEs in the manufacturing sector in Singapore and in the wider region have tended to lag behind developments in other sectors. This has been an historic challenge; as Singapore's Strategic Economic Plan published in 1991 noted:

The domestic sector has unfortunately not benefitted significantly from the influx of foreign investments, which bring it the latest technology and management methods. Upgrading of this sector has been significantly below that of the internationally-oriented sector...

(Government of Singapore, 1991)

Although Singapore is often perceived as a very modern, 'tech-savvy' country, this research discovered that this did not always hold true for SMEs in manufacturing, who often reported that the technology they deployed was not 'state of the art'. To encourage firms to update their capital vintages, the Singapore Government has provided a range of generous financial support and tax subsidies. While the SME leaders interviewed reported accessing of some of these schemes, evidence of their utility was mixed. Some welcomed these schemes and reported examples where they were accessed to upgrade certain machinery or systems to enhance productivity. Others felt that the incentives were too narrow, insufficiently flexible or simply too difficult to access. For Governments, schemes such as the Productivity and Innovation Credit (PIC), which helped to subsidise technology purchases, pose major administrative problems. It is important that they can be accessed without firms incurring too many bureaucratic transaction costs, while guarding against a rapid influx of non-genuine claims. It is also valuable for such schemes to be sufficiently broad and flexible as to incentivise new technology adoption across many industries, but not so broad as to enable purchases of technology where productivity benefits might be questionable. Finally, schemes need to incentivise new investments without resulting in a dependency on what could be described as a kind of corporate welfare. Understandably, it is difficult for Governments to strike the right balance and policy design errors will occasionally be made.

Even well-designed government schemes may not be sufficient to encourage firms to adopt state of the art technology. Firms' technology adoption decisions are often influenced by other factors such as the level of market competition, availability of skilled labour to operate new technology, firm policy decisions taken at corporate head office and the size and value of the market. Thus, Governments wishing to encourage firms to upgrade their capital vintages need to rely upon a mix of policy tools and settings. Here, it is relevant to return to a consideration of Sternberg and Arndt's (2001) model of the nested determinants of innovation (Table 5.1). The utility of this model for policy makers is to highlight the exogenous factors which may encourage technology adoption. These include firm- or industry-specific incentives for R&D and technology acquisition and stress the importance of skilled labour, R&D facilities (such as those of universities) and technology transfer facilities. Moreover, as Griffith, Harrison

Table 5.1 Nested determinants of innovation

Firm-specific determinants impacting firm's innovation behaviour

Industry, market position	Financial resources
Organisational status	Managerial attitudes
R&D capabilities	Innovation networks
Competencies of staff	

Exogenous factors impacting firms' innovation behaviour

Intraregional determinants (location and regional factors)	Outside the firm (technology and innovation policy)	Extra-regional determinants (overall firm environment)
Qualified local labour	Incentives for	Industry performance and
R&D facilities	greater R&D	development
Technology transfer facilities	efforts	Market and demand
Infrastructure	Incentives for R&D	development
Regional economic	in new fields	Competitiveness
structures	Incentives for R&D	globalisation and
	cooperation	Regionalisation
		technological progress

Source: Based on Sternberg and Arndt (2001)

and van Reenen (2006) contend, the geographical location of R&D is an important determinant in the transfer and diffusion of knowledge and technology. Through their various planning agencies, Governments can have a large influence on this spatial dimension of innovation and technology transfer by developing hi-technology precincts and co-locating firms within the same value-chain.

Governments can gain considerable benefits from a greater technology uptake by manufacturers. A study by Microsoft and IDC Asia Pacific in 2018 found that GDP in the Asia Pacific could grow by US$387 billion by 2021 if manufacturing firms embraced digital transformation. The study noted that such digital transformation could include big data analytics to aid manufacturing, machine learning and the Internet-of-Things (Microsoft & IDC Asia/Pacific, 2018).

Managers in SME firms have certain advantages over managers in larger firms. SMEs tend to be less bureaucratic, more flexible, and possess less managerial specialisation. On the other hand, their resources tend to be more limited, their knowledge of the availability of technology only partial, while larger organisations often have the scale and access to larger markets, which facilitate technology adoption.

With these advantages and constraints in mind, what can managers of SMEs in manufacturing do to enhance productivity? Based on the literature review and discussions with experts, it is clear that SMEs need to continuously assess the range of technological solutions available to them. Due to their limited resources, identifying best practice technology solutions might best be undertaken in collaboration with an external consultant or technology partner. Trade associations and certain government agencies can also provide useful information on best practice technologies and sometimes will provide consultants to work with SMEs on structured programmes of technology adoption.

For manufacturers, the trend towards greater and more sophisticated forms of automation is essential to retain competitiveness. This requires SMEs to consider more advanced automated production processes, with a greater reliance on robotic manufacturing technology, CNC machines, and implementing enterprise planning programmes. A gradual shift to more mechanised and automated production solutions will improve economies of scale, reduce down-time and human error and ultimately improve productivity. Moreover, technologies such as cloud-based computing platforms and the Internet-of-Things can help monitor data and vital information in real time, providing a manager with oversight of the entire production process (remotely if necessary) and enabling improvements in efficiency. Increasingly, manufacturing is steadily being transformed by additive manufacturing processes as well as machine learning systems that learn from errors and improve production processes without human intervention. Both of these emerging technologies are falling in price and increasing in sophistication, and are likely to have broad ranging effects on SMEs.

5.2 Improving pay and performance management

An energised and engaged workforce is crucial to firm success and is strongly correlated with enhanced productivity and innovation. As Singapore's Deputy Prime Minister and Minister for Finance, Tharman Shanmugaratnam, noted in a budget speech delivered in 2015:

> Employers must recognise what the best companies have found: that people are their biggest opportunity. Every employer must look for the potential in their people and put time and effort into developing this potential with them. It also means looking out for mid-career Singaporeans who are temporarily dislocated, and helping them to get back in, get re-trained where necessary, and contribute their worth. And it matters greatly too when employees are empowered.
>
> (Government of Singapore, 2015)

For policy makers, much can be done to encourage employers to invest in their own people to raise productivity and innovation. Through its statutory powers, the State can establish a regulatory framework for the labour market, which encourages and rewards firms for developing inclusive, collaborative workplaces, where employers seek to invest in skill formation and reward staff appropriately. Through its role as a major employer, the State can lead innovative approaches to managing employees and serve as a role model to the private sector. Singapore's whole of Government 'Skills Future' strategy is a good example of the kind of policy setting that can aid skill formation – a key element of high performance work systems. Higher Education and Skills Minister, Ong Ye Kung, speaking at the Future Economy Forum, remarked:

> We will need to keep our skills updated, in sync with the evolving opportunities and demands of the workplace. At the same time, we have to make every person count, with productivity, skills and innovation being the key drivers of growth for our future. In this, Singapore starts from a strong position. We have built up the capability of our workforce on a solid foundation of education and training. Singapore has also responded decisively through national initiatives like Skills Future.

(Government of Singapore, 2018)

For managers, it is useful to think about pay and performance management in the context of creating High Performance Work Systems (HPWS). As noted earlier, HPWS are broad human resource management and work practices that are designed to improve labour productivity and organisational performance. Employees are rewarded and incentivised, while being given opportunities and discretion in their work practices to engage in innovative practices. Pay and performance management therefore is a vital component to developing HPWS and improving productivity.

Formal performance appraisal systems across all occupational levels, including production workers and line managers, are essential for taking stock and identifying performance and development opportunities and challenges. It serves as a tool to help both employees and line managers work through a structured plan to address specific performance-related challenges. A common trait of highly productive firms is that they typically rely on a calibrated mix of monetary and non-monetary incentives to motivate their staff. Well managed firms also ensure that line managers hold regular performance conversations to provide their staff with feedback. Best practice firms also incentivise staff through performance bonuses and reward them for working flexibly across a range of tasks, working in teams, and for coming up with ideas to improve the business. To achieve these outcomes, SMEs without full-time Human Resource Managers can consider working with human resource specialist consultants to establish appropriate HR systems and processes.

To promote best practices in firms, SPRING Singapore put in place a HR Shared Services Programme from which SMEs could benefit. This programme enables firms to engage HR experts via consultancies or in-company placement to support creating new HR processes relating to recruitment, performance appraisal, compensation and benefits, training and development. In some cases, for instance with Teo Garments – a retail firm, this programme helped streamline the annual performance appraisal system and catalysed the creation of a new employee handbook (Government of Singapore, 2018)

5.3 Improving training, development (T&D) and organisational learning

Besides updating their technology vintages to enhance total factor productivity, it is critical that firms develop and upgrade their human capital. This has proved to be particularly relevant in the Singapore context. A White Paper released by the Government of Singapore in 2013 highlighted that by 2030 about two-thirds of Singaporeans will hold PMET (Professional, Managerial, Executive and Technical) jobs (Government of Singapore, 2013). To support this growth in white collar employment, the Singapore Government has undertaken massive investment in human capital with a focus on continually upgrading the skills of the labour force. Singapore's Skills Future policy is perhaps the most comprehensive and largest-scale approach to skill formation in South East Asia. The multi-pronged, whole of government strategy invests billions of dollars to upgrade the skills (rather than qualifications) of Singapore's labour force. As Singapore's Prime Minister remarked in 2014:

> Employers must seek constantly to improve their operations, recognise their workers' skills and value and train workers. ...Education and training institutions have to equip workers with the relevant skills. ... Workers themselves must hone and upgrade their skills, as well as help to identify problems at work and improve work processes.
>
> (Government of Singapore, 2014)

In this context, employers can play a crucial role. Ensuring that employees have the requisite skills, and are up to date with the latest technology, solutions, and practices within their industrial sub-sector, is an essential pre-requisite to improve productivity and foster innovation. To enable this, the workforce must undertake regular training and development courses to ensure that they keep abreast of cutting-edge developments and practices within their industrial sub-sector. T&D is particularly relevant in the manufacturing sector, given the nature of occupational hazards and the emphasis on safety and quality control. These activities improve technical competence amongst employees and contribute to organisational effectiveness and the building of a culture of institutional learning.

Despite the consensus of the value of training and development in manufacturing, the results show that the average number of training days (approximately two per annum) provided by Singapore manufacturing firms is poor by international and sectoral standards. This may be as a result of a high dependency on foreign labour, but manufacturing leaders spoke about their challenge in releasing staff for training, because of the perceived productivity loss that this downtime might generate. This suggests that training may need to be delivered in more novel ways, such as via mobile platforms.

In addition, the workforce must have a structured career pathway that recognises employee performance, skill acquisition and initiative, and enables their advancement. Clear and coherent training and development strategies, which emphasise both technical and soft skills, support the creation of an environment that fosters innovation and innovative practices. A holistic approach helps to achieve improved skills and organisational learning and requires employers (SMEs in this case) working with education and training institutions, while employees have to become active participants identifying areas on improving productivity effectiveness. Firms take the 'next step' by identifying skill deficits and examining pre- and post-productivity impacts of investments in T&D.

5.4 Improving innovation culture

Building a culture of innovation across businesses in different sectors is essential and embodied in Singapore's growth and development strategy. Indeed, the Report of the Committee of Singapore's Competitiveness highlighted:

> Given our limited resources, Singapore has to compete on the basis of capabilities rather than costs...As competition intensifies, Singapore needs to continually move up the technological and capabilities ladder.
> (Government of Singapore, 1998)

In 2014, the importance of innovation across businesses and industry sectors was again underscored by the Prime Minister:

> Innovation does not have to be rocket-science, but companies must be willing to relook at how things are done. We will continue to work with

employers and unions in all industries to raise their productivity – not just through technology, but also by transforming business processes, management, and business models.

(Government of Singapore, 2014)

Further, the Singapore authorities acknowledge that educational institutions – universities and polytechnics, alike are a key mechanism for driving innovation in firms, particularly in their ability to connect firms and partners in demand markets in the region and globally. To see this partnership through to fruition, the government called on the establishment of a Global Innovation Alliance.

There is a consensus amongst policy makers throughout South East Asia that adopting innovative practices is key to improving productivity and ensuring that businesses remain competitive. Innovative business practices allow businesses to retain their cost competitiveness and provide flexibility to respond to challenges in the business environment. However, the State's role in building a culture of innovation amongst firms beyond the rhetorical level is challenging. In the context of Singapore, Government agencies have tried to lead cultural change through a cocktail of initiatives that have included establishing innovation precincts, encouraging closer ties with research institutions, and providing generous tax incentives for research and innovation.

Innovations in products, processes or business models are also linked to the R&D activities conducted by firms. Academic studies have long recognised the importance of a bottom-up innovation process in the manufacturing sector, wherein employees generate ideas and innovative practices to improve their business. To enable this, a culture that allows employees to get together and discuss challenges related to quality, production processes, and service delivery ought to be encouraged. 'Kaizen' or 'continuous improvement' that allows for low cost incremental improvements driven by employees rather than a top-down approach should be encouraged.

Effective communication strategies to ensure that senior management listens to employees (through, for example, attitude surveys, open door policies, suggestion schemes, and newsletters) are vital to building an innovation culture. For instance, employees could be encouraged to actively discuss various aspects of the production process together with a view to identifying bottlenecks and improving production and service delivery.

Providing employees with a degree of discretion for them to experiment and come up with new ideas to improve the business is essential in building an innovative company. Tolerating risks, and even failure, in the context of experimentation can be a necessary component of such a stratagem. Firms that recognise and allow for continuous experimentation might also nominate an innovation champion(s) to spur activity across the organisation. Managers might also collaborate with other businesses and research centres to develop new products or processes. The conscious development of an appetite for experimentation, discretion, and risk-taking will facilitate and sustain innovation and help firms to foster competitive advantage.

5.5 Improving government policy and regulation

Singapore has experienced robust economic growth and continuously increased per capita incomes over the past four decades. Many scholars have attributed this to its growth and development strategy. Singapore is now well integrated with global capital and financial markets and plays a pivotal role in global supply chains. Its Free Trade Agreements (FTAs) and business regulation have enabled it to be a hub for business and commerce. In recent years, the nation has faced many challenges in the aftermath of the global economic slowdown and has placed renewed emphasis on increasing the share of manufacturing to national income, as well as improving productivity and energising the manufacturing space. As the Minister for Finance highlighted in 2008:

> We have been aided by a favourable global environment...This is not a story of an old economy growing quickly, but of a new economy emerging out of the old. It is about how we are attracting new and cutting-edge investments, capitalising on opportunities in new growth industries and markets abroad, upgrading our workers' skills and competing at an advantage.
>
> (Government of Singapore, 2008)

Consequently, the Singapore Government through its Committee on the Future Economy (CFE) comprising of industry and government leaders have since focused on key pillars to future proof the economy. These pillars include corporate capabilities and innovation, jobs and skills, growth industries and markets (Government of Singapore, 2008).

Singapore often takes a collaborative approach to productivity improvement, not always evident in other countries, by working within a tradition of tri-partism – that is, employers, government and unions working to improve industry together. Another unique characteristic is the willingness to intervene at an industry level to steer microeconomic reform. For example, Singapore's Ministry of Trade and Industry has developed an Industry Transformation Programme worth in excess of S$4.5 billion. Under this programme, 23 industries have been identified for transformation, including support for innovation, internationalisation and upgrading and deepening of skills. Underpinning the reform efforts is a partnership approach between government, firms, trade associations and unions (MTI, 2018). Given the success of Singapore's reform efforts, it is a model worth emulating in other parts of the region.

A wide range of financial incentives have been made available for businesses to engage with the Government's restructuring agenda. These schemes are managed through SPRING, Singapore (now known as Enterprise Singapore). Some examples of schemes that were in place in 2016 are summarised below. SMEs are regularly encouraged to discuss their specific needs with a consultant at Enterprise Singapore or through a relevant trade association to help them select from the following schemes to embark on a journey to improved productivity and innovation practices:

- **STP** – SMEs Talent Programme – provides for funding to recruit fresh graduates from vocational institutes – up to 70% of pay for 2 years (and includes training and education support).
- **ICV** – Innovation and Capability Vouchers – up to 8 vouchers (each of $5000) to improve capabilities in productivity, HRM, financial management and innovation.
- **iSPRINT** – Increase SME Productivity with Infocomm Adoption and Transformation – 70% of expenses to improve (ceiling at $2000) and transform ($20,000) business practices.
- **IPG – ICT for productivity and growth** – matching funding for using wireless and monthly subscription equipment.
- **PIC** – Productivity and Innovation Credit – 60% cash rebate or 400% tax rebate on up to S$100,000 on 6 areas: IT and automation, R&D, training, buying IPRs, registering IPRs, and approved design projects.
- **WCS** – Wage Credit Scheme – pays for 40% of annual wage increments for qualified SME employees who earn a gross wage of $4000 or below.
- **Other schemes**: Enhanced Training, Work Pro, Market Readiness Assistance Grant, Micro Loan Programme.

The challenge for management is often to navigate such schemes and to take advantage of the broader support that is available to SMEs. This is especially challenging in the SME context because management is often stretched across competing priority areas and they may not have the expertise or time to determine which scheme is most appropriate or likely to yield the best results. Thus, it is important for SMEs to seek advice from trade or employer associations as well as small business advisory services.

Another practical measure management can consider is to cluster and collaborate with other SME leaders to form more effective lobbying groups and to advance common interests. In Singapore, SME manufacturers are typically members of one or more trade associations, such as the Singapore Manufacturers Federation. However, other less mature countries in the region without such groups may wish to seize the opportunity to form alliances to represent their interests in trade negotiations, policy formation and law making.

5.6 Improving leadership and management quality

Leadership and management are vital in promoting productivity and cultivating innovation in firms. As our earlier review of the literature confirmed, sustained improvements in the quality of management are associated with improved organisational performance and labour productivity. A strong vision and business strategy, clearly identified operational targets, regular performance conversations and employee engagement are examples of practices that improve organisational effectiveness and productivity.

According to Schwartz and Porath (2014), leaders who model sustainable work practices in the workplace have employees who are better engaged at work (55%), more satisfied (77%) and live healthier lives (72%). Further, international research has shown that authentic leadership, where leaders are able to guide organisations to achieve their vision in the face of uncertainty and complex situations, highly correlates with management-orientated and people-orientated cultures in HPWS (Boedker, Vidgen, Meagher, Cogin, Mouritsen and Runnalls, 2011).

For policy makers, it is an important first step to acknowledge the critical role played by leadership in promoting productivity improvement and, in doing so, consider investing to assist firms to develop leadership talent. This might include establishing leadership training institutes or providing support for universities to provide such training. Firms might also be provided with tax-deduction benefits when they invest in leadership development of their key staff. Another novel approach taken by the authorities in Singapore is referred to as the SME Talent Programme, in which graduates are provided with attractive salaries subsidised by the government in exchange for working in a manufacturing SME while also undertaking training. The ambition of this scheme is to see talented young graduates develop into the manufacturing leaders of tomorrow.

In this empirical study, many SME leaders acknowledged that leadership was critical for the 'vision and strategy' of the firm and for influencing productivity and innovation efforts. For their managers, leaders expressed a need for analytical problem solving, careful monitoring of staff performance and the active promotion of productivity improvements. However, this consensus was not always supported by consistent action. For instance, many leaders reported that only top performing employees were 'identified, developed and promoted'. Relatedly, our review of the literature found that firms need to create an environment where best practices to improve productivity and innovation are actively pursued and where top-performing employees are regularly identified, developed, promoted and retained. This study found that over 33% of SME leaders reported that no formal performance appraisal systems were used to guide employees work performance. With this gap existing between best practice and leadership action, a common theme across all sub-sectors rightfully identified the difficulty in cultivating senior management talent and reproducing leadership. Thus, it is important that firms actively identify leadership deficits across the workforce and develop individualised plans to address these deficits. Developing internal career ladders in which leadership talent is actively cultivated is also key to driving long-term productivity and innovation improvements. While these efforts require investments in human capital, more sophisticated firms can measure the impact of specific investments in 'leadership' on firm productivity and financial results.

5.7 Conclusions

The key results from this empirical study across the drivers of TFP may surprise some international readers, or even be the cause for pessimism for some Singaporean readers. However, the gaps, weaknesses and deficits observed represent a real opportunity for SMEs within manufacturing to gain considerable productivity gains by implementing relatively modest changes at little cost. For example, implementing performance management systems that identify and act on under-performers and reward high-achievers is a managerial task that can be implemented at low cost, but with a significant potential upside. Similarly, conducting a skills-gap analysis to see whether production staff have the necessary skills to take full advantage of the functionality of machinery is likely to reveal significant opportunities. Moreover, listening to employees and allowing them to have a genuine say in the workplace might well generate useful ideas that can improve the production process and help build an innovation culture.

For firms prepared to make calculated investments, the productivity dividends may be higher still. For instance, targeted investments in training and development beyond the average are likely to keep employees' technical and soft skills at a level that will enhance productivity. Similarly, the deficits revealed in relation to management training assume that executive education is not a priority, yet the extant research reveals otherwise. Studies referred to in this book have shown that improving the quality of management can have a measurable impact on productivity and innovation.

Interestingly, these findings point to opportunities for improvement in adopting technological solutions that may expand a firm's production frontier. There seems to be a fairly limited penetration of high technology amongst SMEs in Singapore, although there are sub-sector exceptions. This may point to the need for greater uptake of government support and grants, such as Singapore's Productivity and Innovation Credit (PIC) scheme. A related challenge is for leaders of SMEs to keep abreast of the latest technologies that can assist them to drive productivity. SME leaders face considerable competing demands on their time and may be unable to keep up to date with these developments. Trade Associations, like the Singapore Manufacturing Federation, consultants and government agencies, can therefore play a strong supportive role in connecting SMEs to the latest technology in their sub-sector.

Interestingly, the results showed only limited engagement between SMEs and higher education and research institutes. This may not be surprising, but it represents a considerable opportunity, given the vibrant and world-class universities in Singapore and the extremely well-regarded A*STAR (Agency for Science, Technology and Research). Connecting industry and SMEs to universities and agencies such as A*STAR is likely to yield considerable productivity and innovation gains over the medium to long term.

A considerable challenge, but an exciting opportunity for the sector, is the encouragement of a younger generation of workers to consider building their careers in manufacturing. Many of the SME leaders interviewed pointed to the difficulty of attracting capable Singaporeans into the sector, because of the perception that the industry was less attractive than occupations in the services sector. In turn, this leads to a high dependence on foreign labour and an increasingly ageing leadership demographic. Singapore's SME Talent Programme, which provides an array of incentives to encourage capable younger Singaporeans to develop their careers in SMEs, is a positive step towards addressing this issue. However, more may need to be done to change the perception of the manufacturing sector amongst the younger generation.

The findings support the strong interventionist role that the Singapore Government has played in driving productivity in recent years. While such intervention might be contrary to neo-liberal economic principles, the results confirmed a near universal awareness of the Government's productivity agenda and a high awareness and approval of government policy. However, there was also a clear sentiment that SMEs were struggling to cope with the changes to foreign worker arrangements, which include restrictions on supply and higher levies. A number of SME leaders expressed that while they understood the need for restructuring the economy in this way, they wished for the government to make these adjustments over a longer time period. Some respondents also articulated the productivity gains that might emerge through the Singapore Government's actions in striking free trade agreements within and beyond the region. This would create economies of scale and help to overcome the limitations of the relatively small domestic market.

Understanding these challenges and deficits is the first step to advancing productivity growth in manufacturing. For SME manufacturers, policy makers and other stakeholders in Singapore and across the region, these findings and the recommendations that flow offer useful insights and inspire a new generation of manufacturing leaders to take bold and innovative approaches in a sector of a fundamental importance to millions of lives throughout South East Asia.

References

Boedker, C., Vidgen, R., Meagher, K., Cogin, J., Mouritsens, J. and Runnalls, J.M. (2011) *Leadership, Culture and Management Practices of High Performing Workplaces in Australia: The High Performing Workplace Index.* Funded by the Department of Education, Employment and Workplace Relations. Sydney: Society for Knowledge Economics.

Faggio, G., Salvanes, K.G. and Van Reenen, J. (2010) The evolution of inequality in productivity and wages: panel data evidence. *Industrial and Corporate Change*, 19(6), 1919–1951.

Government of Singapore (1991) Ministry of Trade and Industry. Economic Planning Committee. *The Strategic Economic Plan: towards a developed nation.* Singapore: SNP.

Government of Singapore (1998) The Report of the Committee on Singapore's Competitiveness. Singapore: Ministry of Trade and Industry.

Government of Singapore (2008) *Creating a Top-Quality Economy, Building a Resilient Community.* Budget Statement 2008, Delivered in Parliament on 15 February 2008 by Mr Tharman Shanmugaratnam, Minister for Finance, Singapore.

Government of Singapore (2013) *A Sustainable Population for a Dynamic Singapore*, Population White Paper. Available at: http://population.sg/whitepaper/#.VPQWYHakrwA)

Government of Singapore. (2014) *Prime Minister Lee Hsien Loong's Speech at Opening of National Productivity Month*, 7 October, 2014.

Government of Singapore (2015) *Building Our Future, Strengthening Social Security.* Budget Speech by the Deputy Prime Minister in the Parliament of Singapore. Available at: www.singaporebudget.gov.sg/budget_2015/bib_pb.aspx

Government of Singapore (2018) *About the Five Futures.* Available at: www.gov.sg/microsites/future-economy/about-us/about-the-five-futures (accessed 14 May 2018).

Government of Singapore (2018) *A Global Innovation Alliance to spark new ideas*. Available at: www.gov.sg/microsites/future-economy/press-room/news/content/a-global-innovation-alliance-to-spark-new-ideas (accessed 14 May 2018).

Griffith, R., Harrison, R. and van Reenen, J. (2006) How special is the special relationship? Using the Impact of US R&D spillovers on UK. Firms as a test of technology sourcing. *American Economic Review*, 96(5), 1859–1875.

Microsoft & IDC Asia/Pacific (2018) *Unlocking the Economic Impact of Digital Transformation in Asia Pacific*. Available at: www.microsoft.com (accessed 4 May 2018).

Ministry of Trade and Industry (MTI) (2018) *Industry Transformation Maps*. Available at: www.mti.gov.sg (accessed 1 May 2018).

Sternberg, R. and Arndt, O. (2001) The firm or the region: What determines the innovation behavior of European firms? *Economic Geography*, 77(4), 364–382.

Schwartz, T. and Porath, C. (2014) The power of meeting your employees' needs. *Harvard Business Review*, 30 June 2014.

Vu, M.K. (2013) Information and Communication Technology (ICT) and Singapore's economic growth. *Information Economics and Policy*, 25(4), 284–300.

6   Conclusion

Despite the nation's enduring reputation as a symbol of economic success, the productivity performance of its SME sector remains Singapore's darker shadow. This research has explored the reasons for this comparative inferiority using a deep, triangulated method and, in Chapter 5, it has provided political and practical advice for consideration by the direct stakeholders involved.

In this concluding chapter, the gaze shifts towards the creation of a dynamic SME sector and one that can be future proofed, if the urgency of the day does not prevent the key stakeholders from focusing on the technological horizon. It does this by first revisiting the objectives and aims of the study and summarising the method, analysis and results. Then, attention turns towards the generation of a web portal that enables Singaporean SMEs to track their innovation and productivity performance against the main drivers of total factor productivity. By using the portal actively, performance can be enhanced as firms employ higher and higher levels of innovation and technology. As ever, best practice is a dynamic concept and populated by the most advanced technology. It will always be beyond the reach of even the most ambitious SME but, in existing – even in the imagination – it provides a powerful motivating force that is constantly progressing. Finally, the eyes turn towards future prospecting through an examination of the workplace of the future.

6.1 Project summary

The project had one main objective:

> To characterise industry performance in areas of innovation and productivity through the establishment of a top 5 to 8 indicators in operational performance and building a good benchmarking database of 200 local SME manufacturing and engineering companies.

Subsidiary aims were:

1. What are the key drivers of Total Factor Productivity (TFP) amongst SMEs in the Singaporean manufacturing sector?
2. How can these drivers be used to understand the state of competitiveness of Singaporean SMEs in the manufacturing sector?
3. How can these drivers be used to develop a mechanism for observing the evolution of SMEs' productivity and innovation?

AIM 1 (and the first part of this objective) was achieved by identifying six key drivers of total factor productivity in SMEs (see Chapter 2) in phase 1 of the research, through a combination of a critical literature search, primary interviews with 20 SME leaders and a Delphi study of international experts. These drivers were:

- Technology and capital utilisation
- Pay and performance management
- Training, development and organisational learning
- Innovation culture
- Government policy, markets and regulation
- Leadership and management quality.

AIM 2 was achieved in Phase 2 of the research through eliciting interviews with a stratified random sample of 215 Singaporean SMEs, analysing the responses and generating results bounded by each driver (see Chapter 4). Finally, AIM 3 was achieved by calculating measures of firm competitiveness for each driver and a total composite score for each firm. Further, an online benchmarking analytics portal was created that served as a platform for individual companies to input their company data, based on the productivity drivers and thus, observe their competitiveness in terms of innovation and productivity (see Chapter 4 and this chapter below). Additionally, based upon the results, the project provided advice for policy makers and SME leaders alike (Chapter 5). However, care should be taken in results interpretation and analysis due to limitation associated with the approach taken.

6.2 Limitations of the research

No matter how carefully crafted the research in the social sciences, there are often a number of limitations of the approach taken. First, the drivers of total factor productivity (TFP) are critical to the whole research process and hence the process of their identification should be as robust as possible. In this study, they are generated from a small sample of SME leaders (20) and a panel of global experts, as well as extant academic literature. This triangulated design should guarantee a certain amount of robustness. But, the mental frames of both the experts and SME leaders represent one composite view of the world. A different sample of experts and a larger and more representative sample of SME leaders may well have generated an alternative view and delivered a different set of drivers. However, as the main sample of 215 SME leaders were comfortable with the chosen drivers, some confidence can be placed in their selection.

Second, as mentioned in Chapter 3, the Gioia method has attracted criticism, especially as the interpretative approach utilised makes the results difficult to generalise. Though in its defence, this is the case for most interpretative approaches, especially if the samples are very different. However, the Singaporean context is unique politically and the nation state is small geographically with a very highly concentrated population of firms. This setting is unlikely to be replicated, even amongst the nations in South East Asia, hence the results will not transfer readily to other contexts without special care in their interpretation.

Third, the Phase 2 sample of 215 SMEs was defined by firms that had been in business for at least 3 years. They would have invested in a certain 'vintage' of technological equipment. In contrast, newer firms are more likely to have invested in a more updated version. Hence, the chosen sample for this project may under-represent the state-of-the-art stock of productive technology amongst Singaporean SMEs. Finally, the sampling procedure employed contained a mix of stratified random sampling and some 'cascade' sampling, where SME leaders introduced the project to their existing network. It is likely that this network was made up of similar types of firms in the same sector, with a similar vintage of technological stock. Hence, the overall sample might be more homogeneous in technological assets than it might have been otherwise. But, throughout the research design and execution, great care was taken to embrace rigor through triangulation, cross-checking and the omission of spurious responses.

6.3 Productivity portal

The second part of our main objective and the AIM 3 in Section 6.1 above were achieved by developing a productivity portal for Singaporean SMEs. The deployment of portals is a well-known strategy used by organisations for data collection, customer relationship management, information capture and dissemination, organisational knowledge management and decision making. In the context of this research, the primary driver for the design and development of the web-based portal was to allow firms to input their firm level data to self-benchmark productivity and innovation efforts in the sector on an ongoing basis. No central database or repository existed in Singapore that captured firm level productivity and innovation data within or across industry sectors. This was hence an industry-first approach to have a decentralised portal to be used by SMEs across the industry to compute their own productivity and innovation performance and benchmark their practices to the sector. At the macro level, the Singapore Innovation and Productivity Institute (SIPI), who ultimately had the responsibility of deploying the portal, believed that insights gained from understanding practices at the subsector and sectoral level would enable them to put in place better designed productivity and innovation interventions for SMEs. Eventually, this approach would mean better value adding to their membership base in Singapore.

A comprehensive process of consultation and design was employed to create the online analytics portal. This included – gathering specifications of the benchmarking portal through interviews with the Singapore Innovation and Productivity Institute (SIPI), government agencies and potential users of the portal; creating design mock-ups for the portal; beta testing of the portal with select SMEs; and the development of documents pertaining to user/training manuals, process flow charts, installation guides and the site map.

Upon identification of the six innovation and productivity indicators – through literature review and consultation with the SMEs – sampling procedures for the benchmark group of 200 SMEs were finalised. As discussed in the earlier chapters, this approach influenced the design of the survey deployed and subsequently its incorporation within the online portal.

The first-hand experiences of the research team conducting SME interviews helped in mirroring the experience to the portal design. The online portal, thus, codified the research and engagement process that was deployed by the research team over the duration of the research. Multiple mock-ups of the portal were designed to ensure user-friendly online interface for firms. A beta version of the web portal followed in the development process, which was tested with sample benchmark data from firms.

The availability of this portal meant that SMEs could enter firm related information on an annual basis and compare their performance against peers in the same industry sub-sector and against aggregate performances for the sector. To use the portal, firms had to provide their Unique Entity Number (UEN) as registered with the Singapore Accounting and Corporate Regulatory Authority (ACRA). This created a unique file in the database and prevented duplicate entries in the portal.

A comprehensive infographic reporting function was designed within the portal to mirror the data collection and reporting process undertaken during the research process. The administrative report designed for the portal administrator group comprised three modules. The first module enables the administrator to query summary graphs for each question in the database. This allows the visualisation and interpretation of qualitative information and data points such as designation of the survey respondent, aggregate annual turnover of benchmark firms in the database and so on. The second module enables the querying of the composite score by sub-sector, by year and by firm. The administrator interface incorporated a sophisticated design allowing for the illustration of the three variables using infographics. An appropriate algorithm design for the computation of the composite score forms the core of the portal. This algorithm also formed the basis for computation of the scores for each of the six productivity and innovation indicators that subsequently formed the third module of the administrative report.

At the firm level, the reporting functionality provided significant information and insights upon which firms could look to create productivity-driven interventions. Firms that reported their data into the portal were provided with a four-page report. This summary report had three sections. The first section provided descriptive statistics which included information relating to the numbers of firms surveyed and the average performances across sub-sectors. Minimum, maximum and average performance scores were represented graphically using bar charts. The second section provided the firm performance related information, particularly its composite score. Two levels of information were provided which included firm aggregate performance relative to the sub-sector and relative to the entire benchmark database. Further, reporting in this section included the performance scores of the firm across the six productivity and innovation indicators relative to the sub sector and benchmark database. Finally, the third section related to offering the firms codified suggestions for improvement based on its performance scores in each of the indicators. For instance, in the *Technology and Capital Utilisation* indicator, if a firm scored around 4 on 10, the firm was encouraged to consider avenues such as process automation, enterprise planning as a means to boost productivity. Similarly, in the *Innovation Culture* indicator, firms that scored a 7 were noted to be in the upper end of the distribution and were encouraged to continuously experiment, nominate an innovation champion within the firm, etc. In a similar fashion, codification of suggestions for performance scores ranging from 0–3.0, 3.1–6.0 and 6.1–10 was undertaken for all indicators, except for *Government Policy, Markets* and *Regulation*. Performance along the scale of this indicator mainly indicated how well firms were responding to externalities, particularly in terms of government policies and programmes. This being the case, while firms received their performance scores relative to the sub-sector and benchmark sample, all firms were encouraged to increase its engagement with government programmes such as SMEs Talent Program (STEP), the use of Innovation and Capability Vouchers (ICVs), application to utilise the Government's Productivity and Innovation Credit (PIC) and similar.

Finally, to ensure firms could benefit from having their productivity and innovation related data in one central database, the initial survey responses gathered by the research team were loaded into the portal. To ensure optimum usage by firms, SIPI brought the portal in-house and deployed it with its membership comprising of the SMEs from the manufacturing sectors.

6.4 Workplace of the future

The portal tool was designed to encourage SMEs to adopt new technology and to embrace innovation for productivity gain, thus helping to stem and reverse a disturbing long run economic trend in Singapore. Additionally, the portal is a future proofing tool that stretches the minds of SME leaders to imagine the future and the associated technologies and their applications. In this sense, a brief exploration of the 'future of work' seems an inevitable conclusion to this project.

6.4.1 Drivers of change

Scenario planners often build visions of the future by identifying drivers of change that work from the past, through the present and shape the nature of the long-term terrain ahead (MacKay and McKiernan, 2018). Because the future cannot be known, they will build three or four scenarios of how it might unfold. None of these scenarios will come about precisely, but elements of them are likely to emerge in such a recognisable guise that enables planning for their emergence possible. In terms of the future of work, it has been argued that three main driving forces are shaping a changed world – technology, demography and consumer sovereignty (McKinsey, 2017), though there are likely to be more. For instance, the powerful influence of the social and work attitude of Millennials is deserving of separate analysis, rather than being subsumed under consumer sovereignty – a variable that applies to all consumers. Broader macro variables like the nature and ease of world trade, migration and the re-emergence of nationalism will all help to sculpture the future of work to different extents.

All these drivers can be considered in an organisation's internal context. Miller's Icarus paradox (Miller, 1990) described how the seeds of decline can be found in the reasons for an organisation's past and current success. There are two interlinked, yet parallel pathways at work. In pathway one, the systems, processes, rules, capital stock and ways of doing things (organisational behavioural routines) become ritualised (semi-permanent) within a particular trading context. In pathway two, leadership mindsets can lock-in on the recipes that caused past success and cause leaders to become over-confident – again, these mind-sets were formed for a particular context. Once external contexts change, both the routines and cognition that were successful in the past are too rigid for change and become tame for the trading conditions of a new future leading to organisational ossification. Miller's warning is useful when focusing on the transformational change that the Industry 4.0 drivers are likely to bring.

The technology driver is critical. Its impact through artificial intelligence, robotics, augmented reality and machine learning will transform an organisation's internal context. Like Miller's parallel streams, these technological advancements are likely to have two pathways. In pathway 1.0, it is likely that they will be used to increase the productivity of the existing configuration of firm assets, within current business models. This increase has been estimated to be in the range of 0.8 to 1.4% (McKinsey, 2017). But, whereas in previous meta transitions like the Industrial Revolution, the impact on productivity is likely to be across all sectors (primary, manufacturing, services), rather than be limited mainly to manufacturing. This technological impact will not be spread evenly across sectors (McKinsey, 2016). Some will have more potential than others to capitalise on these advances, because of the high volume of predictive and repetitive actions (including both data processing and physical work) that they contain e.g., services, manufacturing, healthcare, finance, food and accommodation, retail. While others will be less impacted, because human activity (like managing) and interactivity (the transfer of knowledge and expertise) are likely to remain high in the near term – e.g., education, counselling, consultancy services. Though machines may eventually assume some of these activities (e.g., classroom teaching via robotics, automated portal advice – see above), the substitutability of machines for humans for certain activities, like emotional intelligence and sympathy, is likely to remain low into the medium future.

In pathway 2.0, the algorithmic learning element of technology is already breaching human thinking space, enabling machines to perform cognitive functions. In the medium term, this is not likely to replace SME leader decisions on strategy or actions to create a learning culture. But in the longer term, it is quite thinkable that machines could be used to fortify those decisions based upon real-time remote environmental scanning, big data analysis, advanced predictive tools and continuous, internal asset auditing. Indeed, machines could prevent humans from succumbing to Icarus's cognitive complacency. Through such pattern recognition in large data sets, machines already mimic man's neural networks leading to facial and image recognition, and natural language programming. More important, once machines master non-patterned learning, their ability to create and imagine must follow. Here, bounded gains in productivity within an existing business model will likely be superseded gains beyond current asset arrangements, for instance by imagining and creating new business models through value chain reconfigured and the introduction of completely new concepts of doing business and perhaps a revision of the philosophy and ethics of business itself.

A second powerful driver engages with the changing demographics in modern society. People are living longer, with the concept of retirement being transformed. More workers in the 65–75 and 75–85 age groups are remaining in the labour force than at any other time in recorded history. This increase in labour supply has been accelerated by an avalanche of younger workers from less developed economies. As global changes in regulation are loosened and societal opinion gains voice, more workers – who had been marginalised previously – are being added to this expanding labour force e.g., women, migrants, autistics. Further, Millennials have shown a preference for different ways of working (Deloitte, 2017b), including multiple careers, self-loyalty over institutional loyalty, freelance and remote operating, 24/7 living and gig employment. Hence, the future labour force is expanding, becoming more diverse and much of it has been unshackled from the habits of traditional employment, eschewing boundaries and constraints.

A third major driving force is consumer sovereignty. The digital revolution, smart phone ownership, the low cost of computing power and social media has enabled consumers to gain a wealth of decision-making content, instantly. Such access to information and its processing into knowledge has shifted agency power from the supply to the demand side (e.g., in classroom teaching), and spawned fresh perspectives on organisational performance (e.g., TripAdvisor). Modern consumers have a sovereignty that was not enjoyed by any previous generation. More, such control has fed the demand for customised products and services – customised to one, in many cases. Flexible technology adaptation on the supply side (e.g., 3D printing) has enabled organisations to help cater for such demands. Further, in the employment market, intelligence on what it is really like to work in a particular organisation is becoming more freely available, as ex-employees tell their stories on social media and web platforms e.g., Glassdoor. These platforms give employers and employees alike a much broader employment choice and enable multiple career ambitions to be satisfied. Millennials will be a major influence in the roll out of such technology, with their strong views on control, passion for causes, networking, constant communication and the need for satisfying products and services quickly on a 24/7/365 basis.

Other key drivers like world trade, mass migration and the rise of nationalism will influence the future of work in their own way. For instance, intelligent approaches to migration allow lower cost-lower skilled tasks, that are ignored by much of the local workforce in developed economies, to be completed efficiently. Traditionally, in many developed nations, the set-up and growth of labour intensive, low technology small firms is often driven by migrants trying to establish a foothold in a strange society. But a new generation of migrants is likely to be technologically-savvy, educated and able to bring new skills to the formation of such firms. The latter are as likely to be in coding, gaming and web design, as they are to be in the usual trades of retail or food services.

6.4.2 Scenarios for the future of work in Singaporean SMEs

As these drivers shape future change both individually and interactively, it is possible to imagine at least three plausible and logically consistent scenarios for the future of work amidst SMEs in Singapore's Industry 4.0 dimension. These are TECHHIGH, TECHHYBRID and TECHCHALLENGE and these scenarios might reflect the range of possible futures that emerge in the next 8 to 10 years.

TECHHIGH

In this scenario, world trade is assumed to be operating smoothly, without constraining national and regional barriers. The WTO runs efficiently and proactively. Deals between nations are relatively easy to accomplish. Hence, Singaporean exports thrive, especially along the Silk Road, and inward investment feeds the technological revolution. The nation continues to take a progressive stance on SME technology adoption. Hence, it is possible to imagine a scenario (TECHHIGH), in which the use of cutting edge technology is replete amongst firms. Here, SMEs are voracious acquisitors of data, its analysis and predictive decision making through machine learning. Humans have less impact than machines on the choice of new products and services and their potential markets, the generation of strategic options and the choice of a dynamic and ever adaptive strategic management process. These strategy decisions are linked seamlessly to multiple investments in breakthrough, flexible and scalable technology. Machine learning allows robots to run supply chains, production lines and delivery processes using blockchains and bitcoin-type payments. Through the analysis of big consumer data, products and services are customised to the predicted future desires of demanding customers rather than to their current felt needs. Consumer sovereignty still rules but machines are getting better at building future deals – including their funding – thus allowing a seamless operation of B to B, and B to C chains.

SME workforces are tech-savvy, with soft skills, and operate in empowered teams and networks, in harmony with non-human machines. They work alongside other human organisational teams, who could well have been major competitors in a previous era. Many employees are self-employed and work for several employers and have worked for several more beforehand. Their freelance lifestyle is protected by government regulation and their contribution to a broader society in terms of citizenship, is heartfelt and plenty. Unlike the first generation of freelancers, they have learned to upskill regularly. Their technological charitable work is the envy of other societies, as they support the societally marginalised to acquire much needed new job skills. Their freelancing has allowed firms' costs to be reduced dramatically and their comfortable interaction with robots means that their employability is high, and they are prized as a scarce resource. Monetary rewards do not motivate them necessarily, but they see value in intrinsic issues such as job satisfaction, challenge, autonomy, variety and a citizenship to society as a whole. Such is their competence and fleet of foot, that the government fears that it will lose them to employers in other parts of the globe.

This labour force construct has led more and more SMEs to become far nimbler than in previous years. Jobs have been completely re-designed and are unrecognisable from those of a prior generation of workers. Organisational structures are flat, leadership is dispersed to the teams and all employees are empowered. Because consumers hold major power, firm cultures are marked by a 'can do' attitude to market demand. Their performances exceed sector averages by large margins and returns on capital employed are unprecedented. Future workforce planning becomes paramount, evidenced by LinkedIn passing 200 million members in South East Asia. Singaporean women flock to EmpowerIn, which equips them with the ABC skills needed for Industry 4.0 – AI, Big Data and Cloud computing. Government provides incentives to keep them at home rather than see them migrate to the UK, the USA and Canada.

This heightened demand for skills means that the hi-end SME workforce has to be fortified by the global recruitment of highly skilled migrant labour.

Singaporean SMEs make up the 'hidden champions' in many global markets (McKiernan and Purg, 2013), and they are subject to intense scrutiny by business school academics searching for global case studies of corporate success. The national economy booms through the success of the industry transformation maps laid down in 2018, and any fears that a hi-tech future would endanger job security disappears, as deployment of the new technology, especially on pathway 2.0, creates more market opportunities that lead to a net gain in total employment. Once again, South East Asian neighbours in particular, and the rest of the world looks to Singapore as an exemplar.

TECHHYBRID

World trade in this scenario is a hybrid mix of free trade within trading blocs e.g., EU, but with barriers between blocs and major trading nations e.g., USA, China. Singapore's SMEs have to choose their international market access wisely, with a major emphasis on geographically proximity. Given the degree of conservatism and reluctance for major change in most sectors and in many SMEs, coupled with a Government's proactive technology policy, a hybrid scenario (TECHHYBRID) is also plausible. Here, through its tripartite alliance, the government resolves to increase the uptake of productivity enhancing innovations and technologies. It provides a significant number of incentives, both financial and skills-based. But, firms are indifferent to adoption. Some SMEs become *leaders* and express all the attributes of Industry 4.0 firms. They are run by Millennials, who are serial entrepreneurs. They have a consummate ease with advanced technology, AI, robotics, cloud computing and its translation into new market creation and penetration, with novel configurations of value chains and business models. Their workforces are unbounded, flexible, part time and, sometimes, remotely located. Millennials have made it lucrative for the surge of retirees to add value to their firms, especially in senior management positions, while an AI workforce is developed. They have benefited greatly from the Skills Future Singapore initiative, launched in 2016. This agency embedded the notion of a life-long learning culture within their firms and taught them to benchmark on best practice, especially in Scandinavia, Germany and Switzerland. Consumer demands are crucial to firm success and the desire is always to orientate production and services to satisfy and beat future needs, through the command of advanced data analytics.

However, such firms find local Singaporean manual labour ill-trained at first, and so they are forced to invest heavily in programmes at educational institutes. They remain surprised that these courses are not at the cutting edge of learning, for example the man-machine psychological interface. Their networks are mainly international, and their location is non-permanent. They may move their firms abroad if the Singaporean context gets troublesome and trading conditions start to suffer. Hence, the government intervenes to try and anchor them to Singapore, but tensions arise between the free-spirited radicals and what the millennials see as a more conservative, controlling public sector agency attitude. Eventually, entrepreneurial independence wins over formal bureaucracy and some successful firms chose to move to other locations in China, the UAE, Vietnam and Australia.

Other firms are *laggards* and have stuck with the old status quo as a business model; they have high fixed to variable cost structures, hierarchical structures, time-derived autocratic management styles and a slow decision-making process. They are set in their ways of doing things. They continue to push product and services onto the market, with minimal market research on consumer needs; only lip-service is paid to the increasing sovereignty of consumers. Hence, these firms play catch up and lose market share yearly. Despite overtures from the *leaders* in their sector and within their value chains, rapid technological change is seen as too risky and expensive. They distrust government agencies, who try to encourage and even 'force' them to adapt more quickly. They focus on the near term and their foresightful visioning is cloaked in smog. Employees are on permanent full-time contracts, and many are over the old retirement age and lack continuous upskilling, but they stay loyal to the firm. SME's asset stock is ageing, and it is only refurbished or replaced occasionally. Owner-managers hold a deep suspicion of machine-based technology and abhor robots. At the edge, some of these firms have tried AI in augmenting routine human procedures on the production and administrative sides but, after errors in enactment and worker retaliation, they choose to reject it, before its gains can be properly quantified. The waste of public grants and loans from this rejection is huge, and this attracts suspicion from state agencies and outrage from the tax paying public. Firm performances are varied, and many SMEs remain on, or fall below, the sector average. Consequently, the aggregate Singaporean economy chugs along a knife edge that is cut between the loss of highly productive, radical, serial entrepreneurial Millennials and 'dyed in the wool', owner-managers within its SMEs. Frequent interventions by tri-partite bodies fail to calm the context and so, at great expense, further studies are commissioned by agencies to try and halt the natural decline and re-design the strategy for a hi-tech economy.

TECHCHALLENGE

A final scenario assumes that world trade is relatively free, government policy is intent on state-of-the-art Industry 4.0, and SMEs that show an appetite for change, if the conditions are right. But, they still harbour a suspicion that machines will replace human jobs and so transition is gradual and fraught with problems. A scenario (TECHCHALLENGE) of controlled, incremental growth may be envisaged. The government has accelerated its policy of extensive incentive offerings to SMEs to adopt the latest technology, across all sectors. Sector institutions, firms, educational bodies and government agencies work in close alliance to improve the technological health of the nation. Schools privilege science and mathematics in their curricula, while Millennials help provide technological training to marginal members of the workforce, building future capacity.

But, a lot of SME leaders are ill prepared for transformational change and prefer to use technology to augment existing routines within well-known business models, rather than for the creation of radically new business models. They do not see their own business as contributing much to the nation's Industry 4.0 transition. Change is slow, and government bodies refer to the infusion of innovation into such firms as like 'walking in treacle'. These firms have to be incentivised heavily and, in return for generous grants, their CEOs have to attend specific leadership programmes. Institutes of higher and further education start to fill up courses on the 'management of change', 'leading the innovative company' and 'technology for mature workers' to cater for this new demand. Slowly but surely, many firms recognise the increasing need to respond rapidly to 24/7 consumer demands – which they do using crowd sourced ideas, and to adapt to the new technological environment of Industry 4.0, with its extensive use of blockchain systems, job re-designs, gig employees, highly flexible employment policies. Labour forces become much more diversified than previously, with a mix of skilled and non-skilled worker with age, race and migrant labour – all playing an active role. Many jobs are hybrid, as humans work alongside machines to achieve higher productivity goals. New rules and regulations are introduced to cover these relationships, with the ethical ones being harder for the courts to interpret. Employee training and management education hits a peak, as training and retraining becomes an accepted part of any career, at every level of management. Education institutes do well as their original, multidisciplinary research that interprets the man-machine emotional interface gains ground in the culture of SMEs.

However, as machines learn more, their creativity, curiosity and imagination outrun man's ability, and this results in clashes and strike activity, as employees fight their cause. Robots are smashed in Luddite fashion, inviting state and police intervention. Productivity stalls until the tri-partite alliance can find solutions to the man-robot tragedy. New laws help to soften the situation and the alliance encourages SMEs to invest in a new breed of human friendly, emotionally intelligent robots. The robots are taxed to provide extra spending on societal welfare. Firm and national economic growth is propelled to new highs. Lessons have been learned from the clashes, but suspicion still sits below the surface and human workers remain active and alert. The economy benefits from fresher products and services as firms complete the 'sovereignty turn' in market response, build more innovative value chains and, reluctantly, accept the power of non-human intelligence as a key feature in the strategic firmament.

SCENARIO OUTCOME

Often, scenario planners use their scenarios of the future to prepare strategic plans for the unit of analysis being studied e.g., countries, regions, cities or organisations. They encourage their scenario teams to think the unthinkable about the future and to stretch their current cognitive frameworks into uncomfortable territory. To distinguish these creative visions from pure fantasy, the scenarios are subjected to a battery of tests e.g., for plausibility, internal consistency, surprise and gestalt. Once through the tests, the planners examine each scenario and ask – what is needed in this vision to capitalise on the opportunities it presents; and what is needed to defend against the dangers within it? The lists of actions for each scenario are then compared and, frequently, several actions across the scenarios are the same. Hence, a common set of actions emerges. These have to be addressed, whatever scenario, or part of scenario, might come about.

Such actions recognise that in all of TECHHIGH, TECHHYBRID and TECHCHALLENGE, advanced technology is pushing the limits of human physical and cognitive endurance and SME adaptability. Hence, successful SMEs are likely to be those that adopt flexible approaches to a diverse and changing labour force; that search widely for talent and offer considerable support on its integration; that are flat and fluid of movement; that have a 'can do' culture and an empowered, networked, team-based workforce; and that value the life longing learning of both owner managers and employees. But, it is unlikely that SMEs themselves can accomplish such a major transition from the variety of their current asset stocks, and from the state of their existing mind-sets. Government, sector agencies, financial institutions and consultancy firms will need to play a strong *facilitating and leading* role in the provision of education, training, loans, grants and other inducements. From this study, we identify the Singaporean government as creative in its present offerings, but these may have to be reinforced and accelerated to prepare SMEs well, if they are to extract the full benefits from an Industry 4.0 future.

6.5 Caveat

In alignment with the three scenarios above, stakeholders in the Singapore ecosystem are beginning to lay down the foundations of these technology-led futures in the present. Driven by the Singapore government, they believe that technology developments and advancements such as the Internet-of-Things

(IoT) will be a key enabling force across the different industry sectors. Service-driven professions such as finance and accounting will give way to the need for data scientists and professionals engaged deeply with information technology. Consequently, the Singapore government has set up a *Committee on the Future Economy (CFE)* to focus on five key pillars. These comprise jobs and skills, connectivity, city, growth industries and markets, and corporate capabilities and innovation. Technology underpins each one, and each directly reflects the context of the workplace of the future imagined in the scenarios above (Singapore government, 2018). Driving new approaches to enable the workforce to cope with these futures is a key focus of the government. This is evident in a recent speech by Singapore's Deputy Prime Minister, Mr Tharman Shanmugaratnam, when he said that a new workplace future, encompassing lifelong learning, was needed – a future that developed the skill and mastery of Singaporean workforce, even seniors in the community, to move Singapore to the next level (Cameron, Dhakal and Burgess, 2017).

To prepare for these technology-rich futures, the Singapore government has recognised the need to unlearn, relearn and reskill, which is why it has inaugurated an *Adapt and Grow* Strategy. Under this strategy, it has launched programmes e.g., the Professional Conversion Program, for the information and communication technologies sector. As per the public media reports, the policy approach has started to yield results, with over 11,000 professionals participating in this programme, reskilling and finding new jobs (Seow, 2018). The first signposts that scenarios TECHHIGH and TECHCHALLENGE might be emerging.

If Singaporean SMEs embrace the spirit of Industry 4.0 fully, then the chances of the seeds of decline being laid in its recipes for success should be low. Intelligent robots are likely to develop to sufficient levels that they will make the Icarus paradox redundant. For instance, proactive government policy, dynamic monitoring, flexibility and adaptation should allow machines to prevent pathway one's in-built productivity ossification from arising. Likewise, machine learning should prevent SME leadership's cognitive freezing and over confidence from occurring in pathway two. Negating these influences is the major, 'unseen' benefit of Singapore's full technological enhancement. Icarus may not prevail as a totem of success and failure anymore. However, the lessons of delivering actions for the betterment of mankind provided by the Greek God Prometheus, might be a more appropriate analogy for Singapore's future.

References

Cameron, R, Dhakal, S. and Burgess, J. (Eds) (2017) *Transitions from Education to Work: Workforce Ready Challenges in the Asia Pacific*. UK: Routledge.

Deloitte (2017b) *Apprehensive Millennials: seeking stability and opportunities in an uncertain world*. 2017, Deloitte Millennial Survey. Available at: www2.deloitte. com/content/dam/Deloitte/global/Documents/About-Deloitte/gx-deloitte-millennial-survey-2017-executive-summary.pdf (accessed 20 July 2018).

MacKay, R.B. and McKiernan, P. (2018) *Scenario Thinking: the historical evolution of strategic foresight*. Cambridge: Cambridge University Press.

McKiernan, P., and Purg, D. (Eds.) (2013) *Hidden Champions in CEE and Turkey: carving out a global niche*. Heidelberg: Springer.

McKinsey (2016) Chui, M., Manyika, J. and Miremadi, M. (2016) *Where machines could replace humans – and where they can't (yet)*. McKinsey Quarterly, July. Available at: www.mckinsey.com/business-functions/digital-mckinsey/our-insights/where-machines-could-replace-humans-and-where-they-cant-yet (accessed 19 July 2018).

McKinsey (2017) Manyika, J., Chui, M., Miremadi, M., Bughin, J., George, K., Wilmott, P. and Dewhusrt, M. (2017) *Harnessing Automation for a Future that Works*. McKinsey Global Institute, January. Available at: www.mckinsey.com/featured-insights/digital-disruption/harnessing-automation-for-a-future-that-works (accessed 19 July 2018).

Miller, D. (1990) *The Icarus Paradox*. How exceptional companies bring about their own downfall. New York: HarperBusiness.

Seow, J. (2018) *Adapt and Grow schemes help 11,500 in first half of 2017; majority are PMETs*. [online] The Straits Times. Available at: www.straitstimes.com/singapore/manpower/adapt-and-grow-schemes-help-11500-in-first-half-of-2017-majority-are-pmets (accessed 23 July 2018).

Singapore government. (2018)The CFE Report – Future Economy. Available at: www.gov.sg/microsites/future-economy/the-cfe-report/7-strategies (accessed 23 July 2018).

Index

Note: Page numbers in **bold** refer to tables and in *italics* to figures.

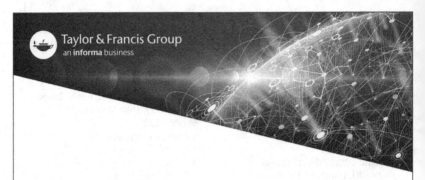

Printed in the United States
by Baker & Taylor Publisher Services

Printed in the United States
by Baker & Taylor Publisher Services